The Indian in American History

THE INDIAN IN AMERICAN HISTORY

Keith L. Pearson

HARCOURT BRACE JOVANOVICH, INC.

New York   Chicago   San Francisco   Atlanta   Dallas

ACKNOWLEDGMENTS: For permission to reprint copyrighted material, grateful acknowledgment is made to the following sources:

ASSOCIATION ON AMERICAN INDIAN AFFAIRS, INC.: Excerpt on page 119 is from "The National Congress of American Indians" by N. B. Johnson from *The American Indian*, III, no. 3, page 2, published by the Association on American Indian Affairs. BANTAM BOOKS, INC.: Excerpts on pages 33, 38, and 60 are from *The Indian Heritage of America*, pages 290, 314, and 133 (pagination in hardcover edition) by Alvin M. Josephy, Jr., © copyright 1968 by Alvin M. Josephy, Jr. THE CHRISTIAN CENTURY FOUNDATION: Excerpt on page 101 is from "Our National Indian Policy" by Harold E. Fey from *The Christian Century*, LXXII, No. 13, March 30, 1955, page 395, copyright 1955 Christian Century Foundation. DOUBLEDAY & COMPANY, INC.: Excerpt on page 25 is from *The Indian and the White Man*, page 173, edited by Wilcomb E. Washburn. HARPER & ROW, PUBLISHERS, INCORPORATED and BARTHOLD FLES, LITERARY AGENT: Excerpt on page 124 is from *The New Indians*, page 124, by Stan Steiner. HOLT, RINEHART AND WINSTON, INC.: Excerpt on page 127 is from *The Quiet Crisis*, page 12, by Stewart Udall. THE JOHNS HOPKINS PRESS: Excerpt on pages 93–94 is from *The Problem of Indian Administration*, pages 3–15 *passim*, by Lewis Meriam *et al.* J. B. LIPPINCOTT COMPANY: Excerpt on page 34 is from *They Came Here First*, page 164, by D'Arcy McNickle, copyright, 1949, by D'Arcy McNickle. THE MACMILLAN COMPANY and COLLIER-MACMILLAN CANADA LTD., TORONTO, ONTARIO: Excerpt on page 123 is from *Custer Died for Your Sins*, pages 62–63, by Vine Deloria, Jr., copyright © 1969 by Vine Deloria, Jr. THE MACMILLAN COMPANY, NEW YORK and BRETT-MACMILLAN LTD., GALT, ONTARIO: Excerpt on page 62 from *Westward Expansion*, page 651, by Ray Billington, Second Edition © The Macmillan Company 1960. All rights reserved. THE UNIVERSITY OF CHICAGO PRESS, CHICAGO & LONDON and THE UNIVERSITY OF TORONTO PRESS, TORONTO 5, CANADA: Excerpt on page 14 is from *Red Man's America*, page 29, by Ruth M. Underhill, © 1953 by The University of Chicago. THE UNIVERSITY OF NEBRASKA: Excerpt on page 52 is from *A Concise Study Guide to the American Frontier*, page 46, by Nelson Klose, copyright © 1964 by the University of Nebraska Press. All rights reserved. VAN NOSTRAND REINHOLD COMPANY: Excerpts on pages 24, 83, and 91 are from *A Short History of the Indians of the United States*, pages 25, 235, and 91, by Edward H. Spicer, © 1969 by Litton Educational Publishing Inc. YALE UNIVERSITY PRESS: Excerpt on pages 15–16 is from *The Travels of William Bartram*, page 326, edited by Francis Harper.

PICTURE ACKNOWLEDGMENTS: Facing page 1, Tad Nichols for Arizona State Museum; 1, 7, American Museum of Natural History; 13, Museum of the American Indian; 18-19, The American Museum of Natural History; 40, Museum of the American Indian; 48, University of British Columbia, Museum of Anthropology; 59, painting by Valjean Hessing, The Philbrook Art Center; 70, Museum of the American Indian; 76-77, painting by Al Momaday, courtesy of Naturegraph Publishers; 85, The American Museum of Natural History; 114-15, Harbrace; 121, Michael Tzovaras, Photo Trends; 125, Don Wright.

ILLUSTRATIONS: Pages 29 and 95, Harbrace.

ISBN 0-15-376079-6   Printed in the United States of America

Preface

American Indians have never been ignored completely in any of the many approaches to the study of American history. But generally history textbooks placed no real importance on Indian societies. Indians were first regarded as warlike savages resisting civilization, and then as pawns pushed about by the forces of the dominant society.

The recent emphasis on ethnic studies, and on minorities as dynamic forces in history, has brought an important change in attitude. Indians are no longer regarded as the victims of an overpowering society. The importance of their contribution to the development of the United States is at last being recognized and clarified.

The significance of the Indians' contribution is explored in the following chapters. Thus *The Indian in American History* is not a history of individual Indians or Indian tribes—that is beyond the scope of the book. Rather, it is a brief history of Indian-white relations and of the role that Indian societies have played in the development of the United States.

After an introductory chapter on Indian societies before the coming of the white man, the three central chapters trace in detail the various ways in which Indians and whites have interacted from colonial days until the present. Chapter 2 describes the Indian policies of the four colonial nations in North America: Great Britain, France, Spain, and the Netherlands. Chapter 3 deals with the familiar story of treaty negotiation and warfare after the founding of the United States and up to the 1870's. Chapter 4 extends the story to the present, through the less familiar ground of the late 1800's and early 1900's. It deals not only with U.S. government policies but also with the growth of Indian political activities. Finally, Chapter 5 takes a deeper look at contemporary Indian problems and attitudes, and at prospects for the future.

Alternating with the three central chapters are three case studies. Each is set in the time period of the accompanying chapter: the Cherokees in colonial America, the Nez Percés in the 1800's, and the Navajos today. Each study looks at what changing white attitudes and policies have meant for an individual Indian group. The case studies are self-contained and may be read independently of the text, but they are designed to complement and illuminate the main chapters.

In addition to the end-of-chapter bibliographies, which reflect the subject matter of the chapters themselves, there is a major listing at the back of the book. Part of this bibliography is broken down regionally to help interested readers locate studies of the Indian tribes of any region of the country.

CONTENTS

Prehistoric hunter's talisman
to ensure successful hunts

1

THE EARLY INDIAN PEOPLES
OF NORTH AMERICA

The rise of man has been a spectacular one. Life has existed on earth for approximately three billion years. Man-like creatures began to appear at least two million years ago. But what scientists can safely call "man" has existed for only about one fourth this time.

Scientific evidence indicates that North and South America were uninhabited by people until about forty thousand years ago. Even in terms of the length of the human habitation of the earth, short as it has been, the Western Hemisphere can accurately be called the "New World."

Long before the Americas were settled, man had already made dramatic progress in many ways. He had invented specialized tools for specific tasks. He had learned to control, and then make, fire. He had learned to make clothing, and he had begun to bury his dead. He had begun to live in permanent communities. By the time man entered the New World, much of the groundwork for civilization had been laid.

However, man in the New World had not yet learned how to cultivate crops for food. He was forced to hunt animals and gather food products in order to survive. Due to seasonal changes, natural disasters such as droughts, and the simple fact that man tended to deplete the food sources in the areas immediately surrounding his settlements, many groups had to wander to far-off places in order to get the food they needed to survive.

For such groups, life was extremely hard. Food was scarce, the climate was often bitterly cold, and the constant wandering was undoubtedly a source of exhaustion. Most of the people who traveled in such groups did not live very long.

THE EARLY PEOPLE OF NORTH AMERICA

The first inhabitants of North America, the ancestors of the people we call Indians today, were groups of such wandering hunters and gatherers from Asia. Because the groups were small and traveled almost continually, anthropologists have not been able to gather much information about them. What evidence there is, however, suggests that these groups came to North America from Asia as long ago as forty thousand years. It is impossible to know the number of people who entered North America during this period. Undoubtedly, it was very small.

Why did these people come? Perhaps a few small groups of these hunters followed animal tracks and wandered into the Bering Strait region. Forty thousand years ago, the earth had not yet emerged from the last of four great Ice Ages, and the Bering Strait resembled a "bridge" of land and ice between Asia and North America. The severity of the climate may have forced some groups to return to Asia, but others succeeded in crossing into North America. These groups must have had supplies and clothing to protect them from the weather and to enable them to survive. They knew how to make fires, and they may have known how to build shelters out of snow and ice.

For some twenty thousand years this trickle of humanity continued. Group by group, family by family, the people came. Archeological evidence has revealed that these groups had different customs and characteristics. There were several different tool-making traditions; and, though these people all came from Asia, there were even racial variations. These hunting groups were independent units and had little contact with one another.

There is a strong possibility that some people may have come to North and South America in another way—by sailing across the Pacific Ocean from Asia. But if such people did cross the Pacific Ocean, they must have made their journeys long after the Bering Strait was crossed. The ability to build boats and sail them was a much later human development than mobile hunting.

Lifeways of the Early Indians

Despite the diversity among the people who lived in North America ten to twelve thousand years ago, there was a similarity in their *subsistence* practices, that is, the ways in which they provided food for themselves. Throughout North America, man was basically a hunter. Characteristically his interest was in hunting "big game" such as the mastodon and the bison. He made hunting tools with long stone points and sharp stone scrapers, and he used several hunting techniques. When possible he killed his prey when the animal was mired down in a marsh or was isolated in a dry lake bed. Men formed hunting parties so that they could hunt more successfully.

But hunting was not man's only method of getting food. Throughout North America man made use of vegetable foods. Trees provided nuts, bushes gave him berries, and grassy plants offered seeds with which he supplemented and enriched his diet. North American man became familiar with melons, cactus plants, chilis, various kinds of beans, potatoes, and, most important of all, corn. However, early man in North America was not a farmer. He did not cultivate these plants. But he did learn where they grew and when they ripened.

This use of vegetable food sources gradually became an important part of man's life in North America, because the climate began to change. Many geologists and climatologists think that this change, the end of the glacial age in North America, occurred about ten thousand years ago. At that time temperatures rose and precipitation decreased. As a result, grassy plains became deserts, forested areas became treeless, and many lakes and rivers disappeared. Some scientists think that these profound changes in climate killed off much of the hunting groups' supplies of big game. Others believe that man himself was responsible for the great decrease in animal life.

In any event, people in North America about ten thousand years ago began to rely more and more on vegetables and fruits rather than on game animals for their diet. Of course not all game animals disappeared. However, their numbers decreased sufficiently to force groups of people who had previously relied mostly on hunting to change dramatically their ways of living.

For example, in the forests of eastern North America man had to change his subsistence practices. During the fall he inhabited the forest, where he picked nuts. In the winter he hunted deer, bear, and badger.

Man made a different type of adjustment in the arid Southwest. Here he adjusted his life to the various climate zones that existed between the deserts and mountains. During the summer months he hunted game in the high mountains. As fall approached, he searched for nuts and hunted rabbits at lower elevations. In the winter he harvested desert plants and, in the spring, grassy plants on the mountainsides.

Man's "tool kit" changed along with his ways of life. Man spent less time in making tools for hunting and butchering large animals. Instead, he developed tools that could make his new life easier and more productive. He learned how to make sandals from vegetable fibers rather than from leather. Fiber was also used to make cordage, which was woven into nets for hunting and fishing. Man made fishhooks out of bones, and from stones he created basins and grinding slabs upon which he could crack and grind nuts and seeds into flour.

Changing Food Sources

In time man began to discover new methods of providing food for himself. At first he simply transplanted wild fruits and vegetables to areas near his permanent settlement. Soon he learned how to cultivate plants, and then he discovered how to raise plants from seed and create new plant strains. Anthropologists have demonstrated that some men in Mexico were cultivating corn at least seven thousand years ago. Evidence of the cultivation of corn has also been found in Bat Cave in New Mexico, but here corn was grown more recently, about fifty-five hundred years ago. Other plants besides corn which were farmed by North American man as early as six or seven thousand years ago include various kinds of squash and beans.

The discovery of farming techniques and the advantages which they provided stimulated further inventions and developments. As a farmer, man became a more settled creature. He now had a certain amount of leisure time. He used this time to build a wide variety of permanent dwellings and community buildings, to construct and maintain irrigation canals and water systems, to manufacture tools, toys, and personal ornaments, and to make pottery and ceramic goods. People began to seek out other groups and to trade with them. This inter-group contact not only provided man with material objects, but it also supplied him with new ideas. Some of these objects and ideas no doubt were later refined and improved upon. The result of these exchanges was a rapid growth in man's technical knowledge in many areas of North America.

By two thousand years ago North American man had successfully adapted to his environment. By this time there was no great need for him to make further fundamental changes in his life style, or way of living. There was land for everyone, food for everyone, and the area was generally peaceful. For centuries man was able to maintain this balance with nature.

TYPES OF INDIAN SOCIETIES

So far we have discussed North American man's explorations, discoveries, inventions, and technological progress. Important as these activities were, they still represented only a small part of the story of the Indians in America. Because man is basically a social creature, we cannot fully understand the American Indian until we examine his social practices.

Anthropologists have divided prehistoric North American Indian societies into three categories: bands, tribes, and chiefdoms. *Bands* were the earliest and most common form of social organization. However, it is unlikely that the first people who came to North America about forty thousand years ago traveled in bands. The climate in the Bering Strait region was so severe and food was so scarce that large groups of people, such as the bands, would have had great difficulty in making such a journey successfully. The earliest people probably traveled in single family units. Some of the units, however, may have gathered together periodically for social reasons.

It seems likely that true band organization did not evolve until a significant number of family units reached the Americas. No doubt the increased food resources south of the Bering Strait helped to make band organization possible. In what is now the United States, for example, vegetables, fruit, and game were far more abundant than in the Arctic. Here several families, not just one, could make use of the food resources of a given land area.

Whatever the beginning of the bands in the New World, this form of organization was very common after the initial settlement of the continent. Bands flourished throughout North America until the time of European colonization. In many areas, they survived long after the arrival of the Europeans. When English, Dutch, and Swedish colonists met Indians along the eastern seaboard, they met representatives of band groups. Contacts with band groups were also made by the Spanish along the Gulf Coast and the Pacific Coast and by the French in southern Canada and other parts of North America.

CUSTOMS OF THE BANDS

The bands were widely scattered throughout the North American continent. Because each group was forced to adapt its life style to the local environment, there was a great deal of diversity among them. Nevertheless, several characteristics were shared by all of the different bands.

The population of a band typically varied from about thirty people to approximately one hundred, although some bands may have been larger. Every band needed a large amount of land for its subsistence. In fact, a band's survival depended upon having at least one square mile of territory for each member of the group. The bands needed such large areas of land because they obtained food by hunting and gathering. Few places on earth provide luxuriant sources of food for man. In most cases, if he does not farm, man requires at least a square mile of territory from which he can get food, simply in order to survive.

The members of the band groups were equal. The only distinctions among band members were those of sex and age. And while these distinctions were important, they did not affect a

This petroglyph, or rock carving, was discovered on a canyon wall in Utah. The figures are believed to have been scratched into the rock by cliff-dwelling Indians.

person's social status. All men performed one set of tasks, and all women another. Basically, men hunted game, and women gathered and prepared food. Each adult was expected to make the tools he needed to perform his work. Time was so precious and the need for food was so great that no band could afford the luxury of a specialist such as a toolmaker.

There was no concept of property ownership in the band. Band members were expected to share their goods. And they felt that the earth belonged to all men equally; no one had the right to own a portion of it all by himself.

Many bands had leaders, but the power of their leaders was far from absolute. Band leaders did not rule, and they did not administer justice. Among the Crow Indians, for example, the leader's main functions were to supervise the annual buffalo hunt and to inform the other band members of important news. His authority was minimal.

All societies are forced to make decisions. Band groups ordinarily made unanimous decisions. If someone in a band disagreed with his fellow members, he was usually warned to conform. If he persisted in his opposition, punishment would probably follow. Band groups were in many respects extremely conservative organizations. They did not change or accept change readily.

Usually only one group member was thought to have special powers. He was the medicine man, known to anthropologists as the _shaman._ This individual was thought to have the power to heal and to cure, the power to predict future events, and the ability to interpret the meanings of events. In band groups a member became a shaman simply by persuading others that he actually did possess such powers. The shaman typically attended to the needs of a sick person, predicted the outcome of an animal hunt, or explained why food had been scarce or plentiful. But aside from these special duties, performed only on rare occasions, the shaman lived much like everyone else. Like the others, he spent most of his time searching for food.

Another characteristic of most of the bands was that the men continued to live with their original band group after they reached maturity. Women, on the other hand, were expected to marry men from other bands and to move to the band group of their husbands.

There are several possible reasons for these marriage customs. First, most band groups were so small that almost all members of the group were closely related. The practice of marrying outside the group, or *exogamy*, prevented incest. Second, and equally important, this practice encouraged peaceful relations among neighboring groups. Bands were less likely to settle their disputes by violence when they knew that they would be battling their own relatives.

Another reason for exogamy may have been the division of labor that was characteristic of all of the bands. As you have read, the male members of the bands ordinarily hunted game for food. In order to track a large animal, kill it, and carry it back to the rest of the band, the hunters had to have a thorough knowledge of local territory and terrain. They also needed to develop teamwork. For these reasons it was essential that men remain with their original bands.

The women's main duty, food gathering, was also important to the band's survival, but it required less teamwork than did hunting and little knowledge of territory or terrain. A woman's skills, unlike those of a man, could be useful to any band.

In summary, the band was a group which hunted game and gathered food but did not farm. The band's small population lived in a large territorial area. Band groups had no specialists and no social classes. Their leaders had no real power. All members were regarded as equal. There was no concept of property ownership. The division of labor between men and women did not confer a difference in status. Ordinarily, neighboring band groups exchanged marriageable girls on a reciprocating basis.

The band was the earliest as well as the most common form of multi-family social organization on the North American continent. Loosely organized and nonauthoritarian, the band nevertheless evoked from its members a sense of unity, an appreciation of the importance of conformity along with the recognition of individual dignity, and a resistance to change. It was truly a remarkable organization.

TRIBAL ORGANIZATIONS AMONG THE INDIANS

Although farming was far more effective than hunting and gathering as a means of obtaining food, it created new problems. As men began to farm, they were able, of course, to provide food for larger and larger groups of people. But as more people crowded themselves into smaller and smaller areas, the rules of conduct and social relationships that had worked so well in the band groups became increasingly ineffective. A new and more complex society, the *tribe*, gradually emerged. This new type of organization enabled early North American agricultural societies to develop and persist.

Tribal groups, like bands, were present throughout the continent when Europeans first came to North America. Some of the tribal groups, particularly those in fertile areas such as the Southeast and the great river valleys of the Mississippi, Ohio, and Missouri, had existed several thousand years before the arrival of the Europeans. Other groups achieved tribal organization shortly before the European explorers and settlers arrived.

At the time of European settlement some of the tribal groups were the Mohawks, Senecas, and Oneidas in the Northeast; the Cherokees, Creeks, Chickasaws, and Choctaws in the Southeast; the Shawnees, Peorias, Illinois, and Foxes in the Middle West; and the Pima, Yuma, and Pueblo groups in the Southwest. The only regions of the continent in which tribal groups were not present, or in which there were only a few, were the extreme northern areas, the Plains, and the Great Basin of Nevada and Idaho.

Tribes were different from bands primarily because they included smaller social groups within the larger society. Social scientists call these smaller groups *sodalities*. A sodality is a fellowship of people unified on the basis of a socially defined common bond. A family is unified on the basis of a biological bond; therefore, a family is not a sodality. There is, however, no biological bond uniting members of a labor union, a church denomination, or a social club. These are sodalities. A sodality unites people from different biological family units, from different geographical regions, and from different age groups.

Sodalities crosscut relationships in a social group and create new types of social arrangements. They are therefore able to bring together and instill a feeling of belonging among otherwise loosely associated people. Sodalities are just as important to Indian societies today as they were many years ago.

The Descent Group in Tribal Society

The type of sodality most frequently found within a tribal society is the *descent group*. A descent group consists of all the people in the tribe who recognize a common ancestor. Depending on the society, the ancestral figures might be either male or female (but never both). In a society that recognizes male ancestors, all the descent groups are traced through the fathers. In this case, children of the same family are also members of the same descent group, since they have the same father. But the mother's descent group remains unchanged. She still belongs to her own father's descent group despite her marriage.

A man and a woman from the same ancestral line can never marry each other; in other words, a person's mother and father will always be from different descent groups. This is a very logical way of arranging people into groups of relatives. The descent group demands allegiance from a widely scattered group of people. By uniting people from different families, it helps to prevent destructive competition between families.

A descent group limited to a few generations is usually called a *lineage*. A large group, consisting of numerous generations and therefore several lineages, is usually called a *clan*. At both of these levels, the descent group served a vital function. It focused the allegiance of the individual upon an ancestor and his descendants. The descent group thus encouraged a sense of social harmony that might otherwise have been unobtainable. Also, it united people from different families. This sense of unity helped to prevent destructive competition between families. The descent group also provided a system for passing down property from generation to generation. In a male-oriented descent group, a man's property would go to his sons; in a female-oriented descent group, a woman's daughters would receive her property. The system left no room for argument.

Closed Associations—A Source of Unity

In addition to the descent group, there was another kind of sodality, called the *closed association*. A closed association is like a club or fraternity whose membership is limited. There were various standards for admission to closed associations. Sometimes parents could simply assign their children to certain groups. In other cases, membership in a closed association depended upon an invitation from the group itself. Prospective members often had to perform certain tests or rituals.

There were many different kinds of closed associations, and almost all of them existed to meet the needs of tribal society. There were associations charged with maintaining stable relations with outside groups. There were associations concerned with internal affairs. These included groups that served as courts of law and groups responsible for the maintenance of irrigation canals and buildings. There often were associations concerned with religious matters. Members in such associations would be responsible for determining the times when ceremonies were to be held and for conducting the ceremonies.

Closed associations were of immense importance to tribal society. Membership in these associations crosscut geographical boundaries, age differences, and family ties. It rearranged and expanded people's allegiances. Closed associations made tribal society more substantial and more lasting.

The Complex Nature of Tribal Society

As you have read, closed associations had certain jobs to perform. Whether the job was conducting a religious ceremony or sending peace emissaries to another group, the tribe expected the closed association to fulfill its responsibilities. The closed association had to be well organized in order to do its job. The word "organization" implies the presence of leadership and a division of responsibilities. Because the tasks of the closed associations were often complex, a class of leaders emerged. Similarly, a class of teachers developed to instruct new members in the tasks and responsibilities of the associations. The leaders and the teachers were those men with the greatest experience, that is, the oldest members of the association.

The shamans, or medicine men, also were important members of tribal society. Whether they served the society as a whole or simply particular closed associations or descent groups, they performed a number of vital tasks. They instructed the people in legends, urged them to pursue certain ideals, and explained the relationship of the universe to man and society. The shamans provided answers to questions about life and death, about disease, about the creation and history of man, about ethics and morals, and about nature and natural forces such as wind, rain, thunder, and lightning. Because there were many independent tribal groups in different parts of the continent, there were also many different legends and explanations.

The oldest living member of a clan or lineage was ordinarily the leader of the descent group. Tribesmen believed that a long life indicated care in one's dealings with other people and with the natural world, and firm comprehension of knowledge imparted by

The Iroquois believed evil spirits caused illness. Members of their False Face Society wore masks, such as this one, to break the spirits' spell and cure the sick.

one's elders. Since the old were considered wise, they were expected to provide leadership.

Descent group leaders often formed councils to discuss tribal affairs. Since the descent group leaders were old, the councils were composed of the tribal elders. The representative of the oldest descent group in the society would become the leader of each council.

The tribal society, with its sodalities, its distinctions among people and groups of people, and its leaders and teachers, was a far more complex organization than the band. The tribe was able to deal with intricate problems. For example, the presence of leadership and sodality group cooperation made efficient farming possible. The results were abundant harvests and food surpluses. Food surpluses, in turn, left some people free to produce pottery and cloth and to design and construct permanent buildings. There was now time for a shaman, or shamans, to provide explanations of the unknown on a full-time basis. The tribes, unlike the band groups, had a wide variety of such permanent specialists.

CHIEFDOM SOCIETIES IN NORTH AMERICA

The third type of social organization found among Indians in North America was the *chiefdom*. This type of society was unique in that it recognized a powerful leader, or "chief." As described by anthropologist Ruth Underhill, the Natchez Indians, in what is now the southeastern United States,

were ruled by an absolute monarch, known as Sun, who held such state that no one addressed him except from a distance with shouts and genuflections. When he went out, arrayed in feather mantle and feather crown, he was carried in a litter so that his feet did not touch the ground. He maintained a household [of aides] who hunted and worked for him and who were killed at his death along with his wife and any others who sought to be with him in the afterlife.

There were only a few chiefdoms in North America at the time of European contact because conditions in North America did not generally warrant their use. Chiefdoms existed only in the Southeast and in the Pacific Northwest. But in these areas, as you will see, the food surplus situation made the chiefdom a highly advantageous form of social organization.

How did chiefdoms evolve, and what purpose did they serve? One anthropologist, Elman Service, maintains that chiefdoms were the result of an increase in specialization. He argues that in some parts of North America neighboring Indian societies could hunt or grow only certain kinds of game or food. These societies, he believes, thus had surpluses of some kinds of foods along with deficits in others. Service reasons that because both surplus and scarcity existed side by side, it was necessary to devise a method of redistribution. In other words, what was needed was a system of exchange by which corn-growing specialists, for example, could obtain meat, fruit, or fish from their neighbors.

In the band group, as you recall, people simply moved from place to place to find food; in the chiefdom, on the other hand, food products were moved to the people. Such a redistribution of products called for a rather complex social organization. An administrative system had to be created to oversee the exchange of goods.

Features of the Chiefdom

Three important characteristics of the chiefdom were (1) specialized regional production, (2) payment of tribute, and (3) a form of hereditary leadership.

The territory covered by a chiefdom embraced different kinds of communities. In some regions, fishing might be the primary method of getting food because of the presence of lakes and rivers; in others, farming might be the most important way of obtaining food. Communities in forested regions often hunted game. In time, suitable areas were also used for orchards, livestock grazing, and even mining and stone quarrying. Each region in the chiefdom produced the goods for which it was best suited.

The second characteristic of the chiefdom was the payment of tribute. This phrase can be misleading. The word "tribute" suggests an enforced tax. In the chiefdom, however, tribute was generally a voluntary contribution. William Bartram, an early visitor to the Creek Indians, described one instance of such voluntary payment:

[When] all the grain is ripe, the whole town again assemble, and every man carries off the fruits of his labour, from the part [of the town field] first alloted to him, which he deposits in his own granary. ... But previous to their carrying off their crops from the field, there is a large crib or granary ... which is called the king's crib; and to this each family carries and deposits a certain quantity, according to [their] ability or inclination. . . . [The king's crib serves] as a surplus to fly to for succour, to assist neighbouring towns whose crops may have failed; accommodate strangers, or travellers; afford provisions or supplies, when they go forth on hostile expeditions; and for other exigencies of the state; and this treasure is at the disposal of the king. . . .

Hereditary leadership is the third distinguishing feature of the chiefdom. Once the practice of redistributing surpluses was systematized, a person or group of people capable of administering this system had to be selected. The administrators might have been chosen from among any of the following: the most efficient food producers, the leaders of sodality groups, or the most respected religious specialists. However, because the Indians attached such importance to descent groups, the person selected was usually the leader of the oldest descent group in the chiefdom.

The problem of passing power on was often solved in a simple way: leadership would be restricted to a single line of descent. Thus, when a leader died, his oldest direct descendant became the new leader. In that way, the society eliminated a great deal of competition for the leadership and assured that there would be an orderly succession.

The chief enjoyed a dominant, prestigious social status. The group recognized that the leader would have to mobilize segments of the population for a variety of purposes. It consequently assigned considerable power to him. Then, in order to justify the leader's exceptional power and influence, the group usually attributed to him superhuman or divine wisdom. The people literally made their chief a godlike figure.

HUMAN ADAPTATION IN NORTH AMERICA

For about forty thousand years, from the time of the crossing of the Bering Strait until the arrival of European explorers and settlers, the human adventure in North America was similar to that in other regions of the earth. People everywhere had to take advantage of the opportunities present in the surrounding environment.

The Indians of North America, as you have seen, took full advantage of their opportunities. Not only were Indians competent technicians, agriculturists, and artists, but they also fashioned new structures of organized society. Indians in North America, then, were not passive occupants but creative forces, molding their society and ways of life to fit the needs of the world in which they lived. Then, in 1492, Christopher Columbus discovered America, and a new era in the history of the people he named Indians was about to begin.

SUGGESTED FURTHER READING

Bordes, François, *The Old Stone Age,* trans. by J. E. Anderson. New York: McGraw-Hill, 1968.

Jennings, Jesse D., *Prehistory of North America.* New York: McGraw-Hill, 1968.

Josephy, Alvin M., Jr., *The Indian Heritage of America.* New York: Alfred A. Knopf, 1968.

Service, Elman R., *Primitive Social Organization,* 2nd ed. New York: Random House, 1971.

Underhill, Ruth M., *Red Man's America.* Chicago: University of Chicago Press, 1953.

Detail from an Indian pottery bowl

2

EUROPEAN SETTLEMENT
AND INDIAN RESPONSE

"Land ahead!" What satisfaction Columbus and his men must have felt when they sighted land after having sailed so long through uncharted seas. Imagine how their excitement must have grown when they discovered that this land was inhabited!

The Indians who witnessed Columbus' arrival must have been equally excited. When they realized that the visitors were coming ashore, they prepared to welcome them. Columbus described the welcome he and his men received from the Indians as follows:

After they have shaken off their fear of us, they display a liberality in their behavior which no one would believe without witnessing it. No request of anything from them is ever refused, but they rather invite acceptance of what they possess, and manifest such a generosity that they would give away their own hearts. Let the article be of great or small value, they offer it readily, and receive anything which is tendered in return with perfect content. . . . Such conduct cannot be ascribed to their want of understanding, for they are a people of much ingenuity. . . .

Columbus' experience was not unusual. Much earlier, and in a different part of the New World, a Norwegian explorer named Karlsefni wrote that he and his men met Indians who gave them gifts of fox and sable furs. Karlsefni's exploration took place in the year 1013. In 1534 Jacques Cartier, a French explorer, sailed into the Gulf of St. Lawrence. In the area now called New Brunswick, he and his men made contact with Indians who presented them with gifts and entertained them with songs and dances. In fact, most of the explorers' descriptions of their first contact with the Indians in North America reveal that the Indians were generous and kind.

The history of North America before its discovery by the Europeans was not written in blood. There may well have been many skirmishes between Indian groups, but there appear to have been very few instances of extensive warfare. Indian groups— bands, tribes, or chiefdoms—were conservative societies interested in maintaining the pattern of harmonious relations established by their elders and ancestors. Conflicts that did arise were usually settled by compromise.

This situation began to change with the arrival of the Europeans. The Europeans were often unwilling to make compromises with the Indians.

EXPLOITATION OF THE INDIANS

Explorations are expensive. The explorations of space by the United States in recent years have cost a great deal of money. The explorations of the world during the 1400's and 1500's also were very costly. Explorers like Columbus and Cartier were sent off with the understanding that they would discover and return home with precious goods such as silver, gold, and rare spices. But the explorers rarely found such valuables, though they wanted desperately to be able to do so. Consequently, relations between the North American Indians and the Europeans became strained. The explorers believed that the Indians were hiding their gold, silver, and spices. When the Indians failed to lead them to these imagined treasurers, the explorers threatened and sometimes killed many Indians.

The Indians also were frequently kidnapped to Europe and sold there as slaves. As one writer has pointed out, Columbus himself began and encouraged this practice by sending several boatloads of Indians home to Spain. Another explorer, a Portuguese adventurer named Gaspar Corte-Real, captured sixty Indians along the northeastern coast of North America in 1500. A French explorer, Thomas Aubert, took Indian slaves to France in 1508. Cartier, too, quickly alienated the Indians with cruel and vicious treatment. He wrote that they had told him of an area "where lie infinite gold, rubies, and other riches." Cartier felt he should take the Indians to France so that they could tell the king personally. Therefore, in 1536, he kidnapped three chiefs and two adult sons of one of the chiefs. The action was ironic, since these chiefs had encouraged their people to welcome Cartier and his men.

The explorers who mistreated Indians or took them home as exhibits or as slaves probably did not foresee the effects of their actions. A woman who had seen her husband kidnapped or killed by explorers, a child who had seen his parents captured, or an old man who had seen young people whipped and chained could not forget such experiences. These people told others of such strange and tragic happenings, and it was not long before the news of these events spread from group to group.

The friendly, gentle, and generous Indians that Columbus observed soon became distrustful of all white intruders. Ponce de León was killed by Florida Indians in 1521 and his men were driven away. A group of men led by the Spanish explorer Lucas Vásquez de Ayllón were killed as they came to the Florida shores in 1526. Giovanni da Verrazano, heading a French exploratory journey, was killed along with six of his men by Indians on an island in the Caribbean.

EARLY EUROPEAN TRADERS

At first, the Indians probably thought the explorers were traders. Many Indian groups had established trade routes centuries before the Europeans arrived; trade relations existed between widely scattered groups. In fact, many of the early European explorations followed Indian trade routes.

European traders arrived soon after the explorers. In 1497 John Cabot, exploring the North Atlantic, discovered the codfish banks off the coast of Newfoundland. Within a few years after his discovery, English, Portuguese, and French trawlers were systematically fishing the banks. The fishing expeditions frequently led to contacts between fishermen and the Indians of Newfoundland, Nova Scotia, and New Brunswick. Relations there remained friendly because the fishermen were interested only in fish, not in treasure.

Cartier's explorations of the area around the Gulf of St. Lawrence led to French interest in Indian furs. During the latter half of the 1500's, French ships regularly sailed to the Gulf of St. Lawrence and returned to France loaded with a variety of furs. The French came to appreciate the value of permanent trading settlements in North America. The Marquis de La Roche established the first such settlement in 1598; Samuel de Champlain founded trading settlements at Quebec in 1608 and at Montreal in 1611.

It is important to realize that Indian-European trade existed for about one hundred years before the permanent trading settlements were established. During this century of trading activity, many of the Indian groups in northeastern North America had become familiar with European goods and trading customs. Groups such as the Naskapi and Montagnais Indians in Quebec province and Newfoundland, the Micmacs and Abnakis in Maine and New Brunswick, and the Huron, Mohawk, Oneida, Onondaga, Cayuga, and Seneca Indians along the St. Lawrence River had come to possess metal axes, knives, kettles, and hoes, woolen and cotton cloth, fishhooks and fishnets, and other European goods. These groups, in fact, used such items in trade with other Indians to the west and south.

At first there was no competition or conflict among the Indians over the European trade market. There was an abundance of fur-bearing animals as well as a ready market for the furs. Along the St. Lawrence River, at least, this situation gradually changed. In 1609, Champlain and about sixty Hurons traveled southward along the Richelieu River to a lake now known as Lake Champlain. The Hurons were aware that they had entered Mohawk territory. According to past experience, they could expect to be met by Mohawks asking why they were there. But there was no opportunity for the Mohawks to ask questions. Champlain shot and killed two of them as they approached his party. Realizing they could not fight effectively against men armed with guns, the Mohawks retreated, and Champlain led the Hurons back to Quebec.

One of Champlain's purposes in murdering the Mohawks was to demonstrate to the Hurons how easily the French could overpower the Indians. Champlain then proposed an alliance between the Hurons and the French in which the Hurons would act as middlemen in the fur trade. The Hurons would collect furs from as many Indian groups as possible and turn these furs over to the French. In return, the French would provide the Hurons with trade goods and protection. The Hurons, of course, had very little choice—they had seen what the French could do with their muskets.

For the French, at least, the alliance was a great success. The Hurons were skilled and experienced traders, and their well-established trade routes stretched all the way from the province of Quebec in the east to what is now Wisconsin in the west. Every year the Hurons would set out in their canoes from Montreal with French goods and return with valuable furs.

Other Trading Alliances

The French were not the only Europeans who recognized the value of having Indian groups act as middlemen. The Dutch worked out an agreement with the Mohawks. The Spanish established alliances with many different Indian groups. English traders secured the support of the Oneidas, Senecas, Cayugas, and other groups.

These alliances between Indians and Europeans eventually led to the deterioration of relations between previously friendly Indian peoples. Neighboring groups which had formerly cooperated with each other soon began to compete; peace between Indian groups was ultimately replaced by conflict.

The situation in the Northeast provides an example of how this conflict was generated and of what kind of results it produced. The "League of the Iroquois," a loose union of five neighboring groups—Mohawks, Oneidas, Onondagas, Cayugas, and Senecas—worked in close conjunction with the British for many years. The Hurons, as you have seen, were allied with the French. Competition to supply furs for their respective European trading partners led these Indians into serious conflict. In 1649, Oneidas, Senecas, Onondagas, and Mohawks attacked and massacred hundreds of Hurons. According to anthropologist Edward H. Spicer, the League of the Iroquois "was probably responsible for more massacres of Indians and more devastated Indian settlements between 1640 and 1755 than the French and British together."

Similar conflicts developed elsewhere. Encouraged by the British, Iroquois groups repeatedly attacked the Delawares, Nanticokes, and Shawnees. Hundreds of Indians were killed; others were driven into exile.

One other group of traders was active at this time. These were the *independent traders*, men who traveled alone into "Indian country" to obtain furs. They were officially recognized by the French in 1654. Before then, however, they were regarded as outlaws. Typically, in the early years, they collected furs and tried to sell them to unlicensed shippers. Theirs was a kind of black-market operation, and many of the independent traders made high profits for their efforts. While their status was quite different from that of the recognized traders, the effect of the independent traders on the Indian groups was similar. Their success, like that of other traders, depended on the activities of Indian middlemen and the creation of Indian alliances.

MISSIONARIES IN NORTH AMERICA

Unlike the explorers and traders who came to North America to take treasures and trade goods back to Europe, the missionaries came to introduce the civilization of Europe to the inhabitants of North America. For the missionaries, civilization went hand in hand with Christianity. The Roman Catholic Church, and later the Protestant churches, played a central role in the growth and development of Western civilization.

The missionaries felt that their responsibility was to bring Christianity and civilization to the Indians. At first the missionaries were not anxious to be identified with the explorers and traders. They generally attempted to meet the Indian people alone. But when the missionaries were unsuccessful in their attempts to Christianize the Indians, they appealed for help to other sources. A Jesuit missionary's letter to a Spanish governor in Florida in 1570 illustrates this point. The missionary, Juan Rogel, described his attempts to follow the Cusabo Indian group and convert them. As the group moved from forest to field in the course of the year he accompanied them, but he had little success in his work. In his frustration he recommended that

to win any of the blind and wretched souls of these provinces, it is necessary first to give orders that the Indians join together and live in settlements, and cultivate the land to secure sustenance for the whole year. After they are firmly settled, let the preaching be introduced. Because if this is not done, even though the religious go among them for fifty years, they will have no more success than we have had.

The tactic which Rogel advocated, that is, the gathering of Indian groups into settlements, became a typical practice of the Spanish missionaries. They often did this with little help. Accompanied by a few Indians who spoke the language of the Indians to be Christianized, the missionary would arrive and request permission to set up a building. The building, constructed from materials available locally, served as a church. In the building the missionary would conduct religious services, even if no one attended.

As soon as possible the missionary would attempt to learn the local language in order to be better able to oversee the growth of a "civilized" community. He would then start a farm and show the local Indians how they, too, could grow crops. He would encourage the Indians to establish permanent homes near the church building. If all went well, the missionary's work would at this point be complete. Circumstances were rarely ideal, however, and missionaries often had to turn to Spanish soldiers for assistance. The soldiers would use punishment and torture to force the Indians to cooperate.

French missionaries were generally more mobile than the Spanish. Some did attempt to establish permanent Indian settlements near Quebec, but most of the French missionaries moved from group to group with the hope of making contact with as many different Indians as possible.

The Failure of the Missionaries

The missionaries came to bring civilization and Christianity to the Indians. But their efforts were plagued by mistakes and doomed to failure. One reason was that few of the missionaries knew anything about Indian religions. Ordinarily, they thought either that the Indians had no religious beliefs at all, or that they believed in some vaguely defined "Great Spirit."

In fact, each Indian society had its own well-established culture and religion. Indian religious doctrines varied greatly from group to group. But almost all Indians felt that Christianity offered them very little compared to their own beliefs.

The Natchez Indians, for example, were among the Indians who considered Christianity far too simple a religion to take seriously. The Natchez had complex religious doctrines and elaborate religious practices. They believed in many gods, not just one. Each of their gods had certain duties and was worshipped in special ceremonies. Natchez priests in ornate garments conducted long and involved rituals in temples and shrines. The priests offered sacrifices of various kinds during certain months of the year.

The Natchez people also observed specific rules in different periods of their lives. Natchez children were forbidden to eat specific foods or act in certain ways, because the gods might be offended. Natchez teen-agers participated in exhaustive initiation rites conducted by priests and other religious leaders. And Natchez adults took part in ceremonial activities throughout the year.

The Christian missionary, dressed in simple clothes and carrying a few religious books, must have looked strange to the Natchez people. And the Christian missionary's message, stressing the idea that there was only one God, must have sounded simple and primitive to people who believed in hundreds of gods.

On the other hand, Indian groups such as the Ojibwas thought that Christianity was unnecessarily complicated. In societies like theirs there were no special religious leaders—each man and woman was a kind of "priest." God was not far off in heaven but was present everywhere—in rocks and mountains, lakes and streams, birds and animals, trees and flowers, and in man himself.

To these people, a Christian missionary who set himself apart from the explorers or traders must have seemed odd. What kind of religion would discriminate between people, making one a religious man and another something else? Such a religion must have seemed strange indeed to groups that maintained all men were equal.

Too simple for some groups, too complex for others, Christianity was not regarded highly by any of the Indians. And when the missionaries intensified their efforts at conversion, the Indians usually rejected Christianity outright. Indian religions placed no emphasis on converting other groups; different Indian religions often existed side by side for centuries. Thus the Indians resented the missionaries' efforts to impose Christianity on them. Such attempts were considered insulting.

In general, the missionaries were tolerated by Indian groups, but under certain circumstances missionaries were attacked and killed. Indians would sometimes put a missionary to death if he blasphemed, or insulted, an Indian group's dieties. Occasionally an Indian group would also kill a missionary when they felt he and his God had brought bad times; in this case the missionary was regarded as a witch or a force of evil. In addition, Indian groups killed missionaries in retaliation for offenses committed by other Europeans. Aware of the prestige that missionaries enjoyed among their countrymen, the Indians knew that in killing a missionary they would strike a hard blow. Of course Christians, too, have killed for all of these same reasons; it should not, therefore, be considered surprising that the Indians did so.

A few groups were ultimately converted. But, in general, the Indians' resistance to Christianity frustrated the missionaries and often led to the forcible imposition of Christian ideas. Although the missionaries had come to North America with motives that differed from those of the explorers or traders, their activities brought similar results. Like the explorers and traders, the missionaries managed to alienate and antagonize Indians throughout eastern North America.

THE COLONIZATION OF NORTH AMERICA

The colonization of North America by Europeans was officially begun in 1565 with the founding of St. Augustine, Florida, by the Spanish. Thirty-three years later, after organizing several other small colonies in Florida, the Spanish settled western North America with a colony on the Rio Grande in what is now central New Mexico.

England and France were unable to establish successful colonies before 1600. In 1578, the Englishman Martin Frobisher did attempt to land fifteen ships with colonists on the coast of Labrador, but his attempt failed because of storms and high seas. England twice tried to establish a colony on Roanoke Island, off the coast of North Carolina, once in 1585, and again in 1587; neither colony survived. By 1607, an English colony had been started at Jamestown near Chesapeake Bay. In 1620 the Pilgrims arrived in Massachusetts. After several failures during the late 1500's, France, too, finally created a permanent colony in North America. Nova Scotia was settled in 1604, and Quebec was founded four years later.

The colonists who followed European explorers, traders, and missionaries to the New World posed yet another kind of threat to Indian existence. The explorers and traders had come to North America to take away treasures. The missionaries had come to bring civilization and Christianity. The colonists came for still another reason: to settle the land and, in this sense, to evict the Indian, that is, to drive him off his homeland into exile.

The words "evict" and "exile" do not appear in the official documents which authorized the establishment of the colonies. But Europeans were well aware that North America was inhabited and that colonization of it would force Indians to find some other place to live. Most Europeans were remarkably unsympathetic toward the Indians' plight. John Cotton, a minister associated with the Massachusetts Bay Colony, was one of many who felt that the colonists were doing the right thing in taking land that belonged to the Indians. In a sermon preached in 1630, Cotton maintained that it was God's will that the colonists take over Indian land. John Winthrop, too, argued that the colonists could feel justified, because they were going to make use of land that was simply being wasted by the Indians. Whether by the will of God or by that of the colonists, Indian land was indeed taken. It was seized first by European rulers claiming the right to issue licenses and charters, then by colonial officials, and finally by individual settlers. At times the Europeans purchased the land, but usually with trinkets or goods worth almost nothing. More often, the Indians were simply driven away.

Indian Response to the Colonists

Originally, the reaction of the Indians to the arrival of the colonists varied from group to group. In Florida, the Calusas fought against settlers at St. Augustine. But along the Rio Grande, in New Mexico, the Pueblo groups welcomed three hundred Spanish colonists. The Powhatan Indians fought with the first settlers of the Chesapeake Bay colony, but the Pilgrims were treated kindly by the Wampanoag Indians at their settlement in Plymouth.

INDIAN CULTURES AND TRIBES

The location of each tribe is approximate and represents the location at the time of greatest historical significance. Culture areas are outlined in black.

ATLANTIC OCEAN

PACIFIC OCEAN

HUDSON BAY

GULF OF MEXICO

SUBARCTIC

EASTERN WOODLAND

SOUTHEAST

PLAINS

SOUTHWEST

GREAT BASIN

PLATEAU

NORTHWEST COAST

CALIFORNIA

Naskapi
Montagnais
Cree
Ojibwa (Chippewa)
Ojibwa
Assiniboin
Plains Cree
Sarsi
Siksika (Blackfoot)
Blood
Piegan
Atsina
Crow
Hidatsa
Mandan
Arikara

Micmac
Malecite
Abnaki Passamaquoddy
Penobscot
Pennacook
Massachuset
Wampanoag
Narraganset
Pequot
Mohegan
Wapinger
Mahican
Mohawk
Oneida
Onondaga
Cayuga
Seneca
Iroquois
Delaware
Natticoke
Powhatan
Pamunkey
Chickahominy
Mattapony
Susquehanna
Tutelo
Nottoway
Tuscarora
Catawba
Pamlico
Yamasee
Guale
Timucua
Calusa
Seminole

Huron
Ottawa
Tobacco
Neutral
Erie
Menominee
Winnebago
Potawatomi
Sauk
Fox
Kickapoo
Miami
Wea
Piankashaw
Kaskaskia
Peoria
Illinois
Shawnee

Cherokee
Yuchi
Creek
Alabama
Hitchiti
Apalachee
Mobile
Biloxi
Chickasaw
Choctaw
Natchez
Tunica
Chitimacha
Atakapa
Quapaw
Caddo
Kichai
Waco
Tonkawa
Tawakoni
Wichita

Iowa
Missouri
Oto
Omaha
Kansas
Ponca
Osage
Pawnee
Sioux (Santee Dakota)
Sioux (Yankton Dakota)
Sioux (Teton Dakota)
Northern Cheyenne
Arapaho
Southern Cheyenne
Kiowa
Kiowa Apache
Comanche
Lipan Apache

Jicarilla Apache
Mescalero Apache
Pueblo
Navajo
Hopi
Zuni
Western Apache
Maricopa
Pima
Papago
Yuma
Yavapai
Walapai
Havasupai

Ute
Shoshoni (Snake)
Gosiute
Paviotso
Northern Paiute
Southern Paiute
Washo
Mono
Panamint
Kawaiisu
Chemehuevi
Serrano
Mojave
Cahuilla

Kutenai
Thompson
Okanagan
Shuswap
Lillooet
Sanpoil
Kalispel
Colville
Spokane
Coeur D'Alene
Palouse
Flathead
Wallawalla
Nez Percé
Bannock

Tlingit
Tsimshian
Haida
Bella Coola
Kwakiutl
Nootka
Makah
Quinault
Chehalis
Quileute
Coast Salish
Puyallup
Nisqually
Chinook
Cowlitz
Yakima
Klikitat
Tillamook

Carrier
Chilcotin
Chehalis
Coos
Umpqua
Molala
Cayuse
Kalapuya
Takelma
Klamath
Modoc
Karok
Shasta
Achomawi
Atsugewi
Yana
Hupa
Mattole
Yurok
Wiyot
Yuki
Pomo
Wintun
Maidu
Miwok
Costanoan
Yokuts
Salinan
Chumash

Indian groups differed in their attitudes toward land, territory, and property. In chiefdoms, where permanent settlements existed, land-use rights were similar to ownership, and descent groups exercised control over the land which they had traditionally occupied.

Tribes had a somewhat less rigid definition of land-use rights. In tribes, if a farmer decided to cultivate a new or different parcel of land, the unused land would become available to others. Similarly, if a tribal group migrated seasonally, there was little concern about the right to use the unoccupied region. And finally, mobile band groups generally defined land-use rights quite informally.

The reaction of the Indians to colonial settlement depended upon a number of factors: the character of both the colonists and the Indians, the areas which they occupied, the time of their occupation, and the work they performed. The Pilgrims set foot on the Massachusetts coast in December 1620. The Wampanoags used the coast only for farming, and they could not grow crops in the middle of winter. Therefore the Pilgrims posed no immediate threat. Along the shores of Chesapeake Bay, the situation was very different. The Powhatan Indians, like the Wampanoags, were farmers, but they also hunted and fished. In March and April they spent a great deal of time along the forested coast; to them, the arrival of the colonists at that particular time was an intrusion and a threat.

As Indian groups realized that the colonists were not going to honor Indian rights to use the land, they reacted in various ways. Where it was possible, accommodations were made. Indians might change their definition of land-use rights under pressure. Sometimes they might avoid the colonists altogether. As a last resort, they might try to negotiate with the colonists. However, if their pleas fell on deaf ears, violence was often the result.

Between accommodation and violence there was a broad range of behavior. Many of the Indians sought friendly relations with the colonists; they treated the colonists in much the same way they would have treated a wandering Indian group.

Such was the case with Powhatan, the leader of the Powhatans, who established an understanding with the Jamestown colonists after a skirmish at Chesapeake Bay. Powhatan permitted his daughter, Pocahontas, to marry the colonist John Rolfe. Similarly, the Wampanoags did not isolate themselves from the Pilgrims. Massasoit, the Wampanoag leader, talked with the Pilgrims through a fellow tribesman who had learned English from coastal traders. Another Wampanoag, Squanto, showed the Pilgrims how to plant and raise corn. The Delaware Indians cooperated very closely with the English settlers in 1634, with Swedish settlers in 1638, and with William Penn and his followers during the 1680's.

The success of the early colonies spurred more intensive European settlement. As more colonists arrived in the New World, they took more land from the Indians. When it became obvious that additional areas of land would be needed for their settlements, some of the colonial administrators justified their territorial takeovers in two ways. They either offered the Indians payment for their territory or set aside special parcels of land, or *reservations,* for the Indians.

However, the colonists used other methods besides payment and reservations to increase their territorial holdings at the expense of the Indians. Firearms were called into use time and time again, and when Indians were not killed outright, they were often tortured. Colonists from Massachusetts viciously attacked a Pequot village in 1637, killing more than six hundred Pequots. Twenty-five years later skirmishes were common throughout Massachusetts, Connecticut, and New Hampshire. In 1675, war occurred between the colonists and an "army" of Indians from several different groups. In a few months the Indians had attacked fifty-two colonial settlements. This war marked the end of any serious European recognition of Indian land rights.

EUROPEAN COLONIAL POLICY

In the three hundred years following Columbus' discovery of the New World, four European nations developed distinctive Indian policies in North America. The policies of these four European nations—Spain, France, the Netherlands, and England—had far-reaching effects, and it is important that they be examined in some detail.

Spanish Colonists in North America

The Spanish were at first interested only in the treasure they thought the New World contained. At this time Spain had no formal Indian policy, but Spanish settlers did not avoid contact with Indians. Spanish colonists in the West Indies used Indians to mine and to farm, and they frequently mistreated them. A Spaniard named Bartolomé de las Casas published a book in 1552 entitled *A Brief Relation of the Destruction of the Indies.* De las Casas reported many instances of cruel and unusual torture and punishment.

In 1503 Queen Isabella was told of several incidents of brutality, but her major concern was that many Indians had begun to run away from the colonial settlements. She wrote to the Royal Governor of the Indies, Nicolas de Ovando, instructing him as follows:

[Because the Indians] avoid contact and community with the Spaniards to such an extent that they will not even work for wages . . . and cannot be had by the Christians to convert to the Holy Catholic Faith . . . and because this can be better done by having the Indians living in community with the Christians of the island . . . I have commanded that beginning from the day you receive my letter, you will compel and force the said Indians to associate with the Christians . . . to gather and mine the gold . . . to till the fields.

This policy was later expanded to provide houses and plots of land for the Indians. In 1512 King Ferdinand of Spain approved the adoption of a set of laws, the *Laws of Burgos,* dealing with Indian rights. To enforce these laws he appointed members of the Order of St. Jerome, a religious group. Because of resistance from the colonial administrators, however, the Laws of Burgos were never effective. In 1524 Spain created the Council of the Indies and gave it supreme judicial and legislative authority over Spanish activities in the New World.

The policy which gradually evolved and became characteristic of Spanish dealings with Indians in the New World is known as the *encomienda.* The encomienda policy had several noteworthy features. First, because it guaranteed to each Spanish settler not only a plot of land but also the labor of the Indians living there, it encouraged Spanish colonization. Second, because the Indians would be forced to live so close to the colonists, it was expected that the encomienda system would make the work of missionaries much easier and more successful. Finally, because Spaniards receiving land grants under the encomienda system were required to protect their Indian workers, it was expected that atrocities against the Indians would be eliminated. But, according to historian Alvin M. Josephy, Jr., while the encomienda policy was meant to give the Indians a degree of protection for ends deemed purposeful by Church and State . . . it was abused almost everywhere. Despite efforts in Spain to reform the system and make it work, there was little enforcement of court orders in the colonies. In practice, the *encomienda* system merely quickened the enslavement of the Indian population.

Colonial Practices of the French

France, at first, had no official Indian policy. The French rulers simply issued charters to trading companies, and the traders were free to deal with the Indians as they saw fit. Generally, the traders proceeded on the assumption that the Indians were friendly, cooperative, and nonaggressive. Many of the men in the trading colonies, as well as the independent traders, married Indian women and adjusted to local Indian customs. Cartier and Samuel de Champlain were among the many French explorers and traders who were highly impressed by the Indian towns built along the St. Lawrence River.

The French traders also recognized the distinctions that existed among the Indian groups. Champlain commented, for example, that the Hurons were quite different from the Naskapis or the Mohawks. Being aware of these variations, the French used different approaches in their dealings with various Indian groups. Occasionally they employed force, as in the Mohawk incident mentioned earlier.

An official policy was adopted in 1663, when the French king, Louis XIV, assumed control of French activities in North America. Louis XIV approved the colonization program that had been defined by the traders. Large areas of land were assigned to certain individuals who, in turn, would rent smaller plots to tenant farmers. Louis XIV also ordered the establishment of an administrative organization. The system was run by a Governor-General, a financial manager called an intendant, and a bishop.

One reason that Louis XIV assumed control of the North American colonies was to counteract the effects of Champlain's activities in the New World. Champlain, you will remember, had negotiated a working agreement with the Hurons. The French-Huron alliance ushered in an era of distrust and hostility. By the 1640's the French and the Hurons had become engaged in regular skirmishes with other Indians in the area. Member groups in the League of the Iroquois, especially the Mohawks, learned that the Dutch and some New England colonists would provide them with weapons. These Indians were now well equipped to fight the French.

In 1649 Iroquois groups attacked and nearly annihilated the pro-French Hurons. At about the same time the Iroquois intensified their raids on French settlements. By the 1660's, approximately twenty years after the first raids, the French settlers had become demoralized. Few furs were leaving the country, and the trading colonies were becoming increasingly unprofitable. In 1661, and for several years thereafter, French soldiers were sent from France to save what was left of the French settlements along the St. Lawrence River. Peaceful relations were reestablished between the Mohawks and the French. The French were less successful, however, in their negotiations with other groups in the Iroquois League. Sporadic fighting continued for years.

The administrative organization which was set up by Louis XIV helped to create better Indian-French relations in four ways. In the first place, the Governor-General had the power to regulate and approve land accessions. In other words, no person or group of persons could settle on land without his permission and approval. Second, the Governor-General was concerned with Indian affairs. Indians were encouraged to take complaints directly to the Governor-General; the Governor-General was, in turn, responsible for holding annual conferences with Indian groups. These took place at first in Montreal and later, as French influence expanded, in Mobile, Alabama, as well. Such conferences were the scene not only of discussion, but also of feasting, exchanging gifts, and trading. As historian D'Arcy McNickle points out, "It has been estimated that the Governor-General of Canada devoted as much as three months out of every year to Indian affairs."

A third important feature of the new system was the Governor-General's control over trading activities. He was able to direct trading expeditions into certain regions and draw them away from others. Thus, if one area was being overtraded, or if Indians in a given area complained about the activities of the traders, the Governor-General could prohibit trading in those areas. Finally, the Governor-General had military authority, and he discouraged French soldiers from harassing Indians.

The creation of a French administrative system in 1663 was the key to the rapid expansion of French influence in North America. Expeditions consisting of traders, missionaries, and soldiers traveled in all directions to contact Indian groups. In most cases these expeditions were peaceful and productive for France, since they resulted in increased quantities of furs. Frequently, small trading outposts were established. Quite often the traders married Indian women and were accepted as friends by the local Indian groups. Relations between the French and the Indians became more friendly as time went on. In the early 1700's Indians fought against English and Spanish settlers in order to protect French traders.

Dutch Activities in the New World

The Dutch settlements in North America were restricted chiefly to the Hudson River area, Long Island, and the New Jersey coast. Dutch control of these settlements lasted only forty years. Albany was settled in 1624, New York a year later; by 1664 the English assumed control of the Hudson River area and other Dutch settlements as well. Although the Dutch experience in North America was restricted in both time and space, Dutch policy toward the Indians was distinctive in several ways.

During his explorations for the Dutch in 1609, Henry Hudson met the Mohawks, and he established good relations with them immediately. From the beginning, Dutch settlers in Albany considered the friendship of the Mohawks important. Later, as Manhattan Island, Staten Island, and the lower Hudson River area were settled, the Dutch encouraged peaceful relations with Indian groups there.

Dutch colonial administrators were required either to find unused land for settlement or to purchase land from the Indians. For instance, in 1625, reports of problems between Dutch settlers and the Indians reached the Dutch government. The colonial administrator in charge was immediately reminded that it was government policy for the settlers to buy their land, and that land was not to be gained by fraud.

Following this policy, the Dutch "bought" Manhattan Island from the Indians in 1626; and during their early occupancy of the Hudson River area they "purchased," often with beads, most of the land on which they finally settled. But it is doubtful that the Indians who "sold" their land to the Dutch and to other Europeans fully understood that they were giving up use of their territory forever. In some cases, when the Dutch settlers began to build permanent buildings and to farm such "purchased" land, the Indians responded violently. In later years the English created additional problems by encouraging these Indians to repossess their land from the Dutch.

In general, though, Dutch policy toward the Indians was marked by respect and consideration, and the Indians responded in kind. In 1641, for example, a Dutch settler was killed by an Indian near Hackensack. Disturbed by the action of one of their people, several representatives of the local Indian group came to speak with Governor William Kiefft. They stated that they were ashamed of the killing, that the person who had done it was drunk and not in full command of himself, and that they would punish the offender. They also said that since the murdered man had been a husband and father, they would like to help the grieving widow by giving her some *zeewan,* their form of money.

Dutch relations with the Mohawks remained friendly all through the years of the Hudson River settlements. The Mohawks cooperated with the Dutch when they were attacked; the Dutch assisted the Mohawks in their fights with the French. Apparently this cooperation was simply due to mutual respect. And in 1643 the Dutch and the Mohawks made a formal statement of their friendship.

The English Experience in America

English colonies were of three types, but only one was directly under the control of the English government. This type was known as the royal colony. The royal colonies were administered by an English group called the *Board of Trade.* The Board formulated Indian policy and was responsible for the legal settlement of problems between colonists and Indians.

The history of the English colonies in North America contains the stories of a number of honest and conscientious individuals who regarded the Indian as a human being and treated him with fairness, honesty, and respect. But greedy land speculators and traders were also common, and they considered the Indian an object to be used solely for personal gain. These traders and land speculators created serious problems for both the Indians and the colonial administrators. The Board of Trade attempted to control the unscrupulous traders and speculators in the royal colonies, but there was little they could do to restrict their operations in other English settlements.

In 1688 there were about two hundred thousand English colonists in North America. By 1700 this number had more than doubled, and the expanding colonies exerted great pressure upon local Indian groups. The colonists took over Indian land through purchase, negotiation, or force. In many cases the only recourse for the Indians was warfare. War, however, was generally a futile exercise for the poorly armed Indians. Some of the Indian groups near the eastern Great Lakes sought to fortify their position, and they began to join French soldiers in skirmishes with the English colonists.

In 1754 the English Board of Trade became concerned about the welfare of the royal colonies in North America. The Board recognized that the expansion of the royal colonies in northwestern Pennsylvania and Ohio was being threatened by Indian resistance and French operations. A conference was held at Albany, New York, in June 1754. Delegates from New York, Connecticut, Maryland, Pennsylvania, Rhode Island, New Hampshire, and Massachusetts met with representatives of the member groups of the League of the Iroquois. One aim of the conference was ostensibly to work out a plan to protect the Iroquois from French expansion. Member groups of the Iroquois League had fought the English in the past, and relations had continued to deteriorate since then. The English, however, realized that the French were serious about developing settlements in Ohio. The French would have a very easy time doing as they planned unless the Iroquois could be persuaded to oppose French activity. The English ultimately succeeded in winning Iroquois support.

The French and Indian War, or the Seven Years' War, started one month after the English colonists met at the so-called Albany Congress. Colonel George Washington was involved in a skirmish with the French near Pittsburgh on July 3, 1754. After this skirmish the fighting intensified. The French were eventually driven out of the area, and by the time peace came in 1763, the English had become deeply involved in Indian affairs.

For a variety of reasons the English had managed to antagonize many of their wartime Indian allies. Toward the end of the war, an Ottawa chief named Pontiac led a large group that included Ottawas, Delawares, Shawnees, Ojibwas, Potawatomis, Miamis, Senecas, and Hurons in attacks on English positions around Detroit. Though the so-called Pontiac's Rebellion was eventually crushed, the defeated Indians now regarded the English as their sworn enemies.

At the end of the French and Indian War, the English issued the *Proclamation of 1763*, which outlined their Indian policy.

The main achievement of this document was the establishment of a western boundary for English settlement. The country west of the Appalachians was to be reserved for Indian occupancy. Settlers who had moved into the western territory were to leave and return eastward; if they did not, troops would be dispatched to take them back. No land was to be sold west of this boundary. Trading posts were to be restricted to the border.

The intent of the Proclamation was generous. However, traders and land speculators refused to obey its provisions. Frequently these traders and speculators crossed the Appalachians and forced the Indians to vacate their lands. As Josephy describes it,

Syndicates of land speculators, employing prospectors like Daniel Boone, led the way, focusing on the fertile lands of Kentucky and the upper Ohio Valley. The incursions again inflamed the Indians, and various bands . . . tried to push back the whites. Kentucky, which became known as a "dark and bloody ground," was the scene of savage skirmishing that reached a climax in 1774 with the so-called Lord Dunmore's War, named for the royal governor of Virginia.

The English faced a difficult problem in enforcing the Proclamation of 1763 because the officials of the Indian Department, created by the Albany Congress, had no real authority.

THE SURVIVAL OF INDIAN SOCIETIES

In the 271 years between Columbus' landing in the New World and the Proclamation of 1763, the nature of American Indian life had been drastically changed by European activities. Many Indian societies which had existed for centuries before the coming of the whites completely disappeared, through warfare, disease, or eviction from their homelands. Other societies had been seriously weakened by the same forces and would soon dissolve. This period, almost three centuries long, indeed was a tragic one for countless numbers of Indians.

However, it is important to realize that no one, in 1763, was ready to say that the Indians were doomed. Though severe changes had occurred, thousands of Indians in many separate groups had accepted the changes and readjusted their lives. They confidently looked forward to the future.

The persistence of Indian societies under these circumstances derived from centuries of social experience. Legends informed each new generation of Indians of the achievements of their ancestors. Religious teachings explained how supernatural forces waited to help them succeed under difficult conditions. Social traditions united individuals into cohesive groups able to withstand almost any kind of destructive pressure. Leaders, aware of the past and capable of dealing wisely with the future, inspired confidence in members of the society.

It is astonishing that so many Indian societies survived the pressures of European activities in these years. Many, in fact, such as the Cherokees, actually increased in numbers despite the destructive efforts of European traders, missionaries, and colonists.

SUGGESTED FURTHER READING

McNickle, D'Arcy, *They Came Here First*. Philadelphia: J. B. Lippincott, 1949.

Nammack, Georgiana C., *Fraud, Politics, and the Dispossession of the Indians*. Norman, Oklahoma: University of Oklahoma Press, 1969.

Washburn, Wilcomb E., ed., *The Indian and the White Man*. New York: Doubleday & Company, 1964.

a case study:

THE CHEROKEES IN THE COLONIAL PERIOD

Books about colonial America frequently contain lurid descriptions of the savage and warlike qualities of North American Indians. These descriptions are usually based on records and letters written by the colonists. Because of this it is not surprising that many people think Indians were warlike.

Recently, however, an increasing number of studies have raised questions about the validity of the colonists' descriptions. The Cherokee Indians are a case in point. The Cherokees have been called the "warlords" of the Southeast; colonial observers claimed that war was the tribe's main occupation. Sensational accounts of their "savage nature" and "torture practices" were widely publicized by the colonists. But the actual facts were quite different.

When contacts between European colonists and the Cherokees began to be quite frequent, in the late 1600's, there were more than 12,000 Cherokee people. They occupied a large area in the southern Appalachian region, in what are now the states of Tennessee, North Carolina, South Carolina, Georgia, and Alabama. Most of them lived in small houses grouped into compact settlements or towns; there were about fifty such settlements in the territory during the early period of colonial contact. Agriculture was the tribe's main economic activity. The fields were owned by the community, and families were assigned specific farm plots in the fields. The entire Cherokee family worked at farming. Even the children had their agricultural responsibilities.

The Cherokees were also expert traders. They dealt regularly with neighboring groups such as the Tuscaroras, Catawbas, and the tribes of the Creek Confederacy. At times their trading expeditions went as far as the Great Lakes, the Mississippi River, and deep into Florida to make contact with other groups.

Cherokee Society

Women were very important in Cherokee society. The Cherokees traced descent through the mother, and older women in the clans consequently had a great deal of authority. These women had the power to select town leaders and to influence, or even dictate, community decisions. They were generally respected for their wisdom. But although women possessed a great deal of authority, the town leaders themselves were usually men.

Shamans, or religious leaders, were highly esteemed in Cherokee society. The shamans conducted religious ceremonies and ministered to the special needs of families. They also reminded the people of their traditions and the examples of their ancestors. Cherokee legends stressed the dedication, bravery, and strength of the Cherokee ancestors, who overcame difficult obstacles to provide the Cherokees with land and food resources. Shamans continually exhorted parents to teach their children the importance of such Cherokee ideals as honesty, the rights of other people, and bravery.

Because of their traditions and their interest in trade, the Cherokees were not afraid of change. They often adopted new customs or tried out practices that they learned from their contacts with other groups. For example, the Cherokees quickly learned to use European farming tools, guns, and textiles.

Cherokee Political Organization

When they first met European colonists, the Cherokees already possessed one of the most complex, sophisticated, and effective political organizations in North America. The tribe's territory was divided into three geographic districts. Each district was governed by a district council made up of the various town leaders. Each of the three district councils had two officers. One of these was called the peace chief. He was responsible for maintaining harmony among the people of his district. The other, known as the war chief, was responsible for the conduct of external affairs.

Council meetings dealt with both internal and external affairs. In civil matters the councils functioned largely as courts of law, settling disputes between families and trying individuals accused of crimes. In external affairs, the councils decided questions of war and peace and governed trade with outsiders. If a Cherokee town was raided, for example, the council decided whether or not retaliation should be taken. Traders from other societies had to negotiate with the district councils for trading rights. District councils were also responsible for the long trading expeditions undertaken by Cherokee parties.

The three districts were unified by a tribal leadership of three people. The supreme leader, who had to be a member of the most important Cherokee clan, was known as Uku, or "beloved one." He had two assistants, a tribal war chief and a tribal peace chief. The functions of these two tribal chiefs were generally similar to those of their district counterparts.

Though the Cherokee political system embraced the whole tribe, it stressed local autonomy. Only the most important matters were decided at the district or the tribal level. A leader's authority depended on how effectively he could persuade others to agree with him. A strong leader, therefore, had to be a diplomat, sensitive to the opinions of different groups.

Cherokees and Colonists

Three different nations were involved in the colonization of the Southeast. Spanish colonists settled in Florida and along the Gulf Coast. The French explored and settled Louisiana and Mississippi. The English established colonies in Georgia, Virginia, and the Carolinas. The Cherokees, thus, were eventually almost surrounded by colonists from these three European nations.

Contact with the Spanish had begun in 1540 when Hernando De Soto's men entered a Cherokee town. But for the next century or more there probably were only occasional meetings between Cherokees and Europeans. In the late 1600's, however, the number of contacts increased greatly, particularly between the Cherokees and the British and French. From then on, the Cherokee's interaction with the colonists took several different forms. The relationship developed in four separate and distinct stages.

Cherokee Dominance: to 1730

During the first and longest phase of their relations with the colonists, the Cherokees were the dominant society. While British settlers, and later French settlers as well, were struggling to survive, the Cherokees were secure. Their economic activities provided them with ample food; their social and political structure insured tribal harmony; their relations with neighboring Indian groups were peaceful, and their trading activities were profitable.

When the early colonists began trading with the Cherokees, they were willing to accept any terms the Cherokees named. Colonial administrators were under strong pressure to send furs, skins, and minerals to European markets, and the Cherokees knew that this gave them an excellent bargaining position. They insisted that the colonists pay premiums for trading privileges. The colonists, having little choice, were forced to pay regularly.

The Cherokees held another kind of advantage as well. At times the British or French needed military help. The Cherokee district councils were sometimes able to send their men on this kind of duty, and when they did they demanded generous payments. Though both the British and the French tried to persuade the Cherokees to enter into formal alliances, they failed. The Cherokees felt that very little could be gained from such alliances. If the colonists were willing to pay for military assistance and trade privileges, the Cherokee tribe was far better off by remaining independent.

An event in 1715 demonstrates the extent of the Cherokee domination over the British colonists in this period. Through their occasional service with colonial armies, the Cherokees discovered that the British were kidnapping Indians to send to European slave markets. In retaliation, the Cherokees severed all relations with the British and joined with neighboring tribes, the Yamasees and the Catawbas, in attacking British settlements.

For six years the Cherokees refused to have any official dealings with the British colonists. Finally, in 1721, tribal leaders responded to the colonists' frequent pleas and met with them at Charleston, South Carolina. The meeting led to a treaty which was very favorable to the Cherokees. In exchange for a small parcel of land for a British trading post, the tribal leaders obtained three important concessions. The British agreed to stop the kidnapping, appoint a single person to negotiate trade agreements, and continue paying for trade privileges.

In the next few years the Cherokee district and tribal leaders encouraged the rapid expansion of trade with all colonists. Their trade practices forced the British colonists to compete against each other and against the French for Cherokee trade. The situation was as frustrating for the colonists as it was profitable for the tribe.

Cherokee Discord: 1730–1745

With an unexpected development in 1730, the balance began to shift. In March of that year an Englishman named Sir Alexander Cuming appeared before the Cherokee district councils, insisting that he had been sent by the British king to arrange new trade policies. Two of the district councils rejected him outright, but he was accepted by the war chief of the third, a man named Moytoy. In return, Cuming designated Moytoy "emperor of all Cherokee." Moytoy was asked to select a party of Cherokees to visit England and meet the king. During the course of their four-month visit, the men signed a treaty committing the Cherokees to an exclusive trade agreement with Great Britain.

Since none of the Cherokees who had gone on the trip had the authority to sign a trade treaty for the tribe, the negotiations were practically worthless. But this fact did not stop the British from making heavy demands on the appointed "emperor." Instructed to deliver Cherokee trade goods to British markets, Moytoy visited towns and councils, promising them great benefits in return for their cooperation. Some were persuaded and soon began to operate independently of tribal policies. Other towns and councils refused.

The French were equally eager to destroy the power of the Cherokee tribe. In a few years they began their own program of disruption by secretly abducting the tribal peace chief. A Frenchman named Christian Prieber then met with the Uku and the tribal war chief and suggested that they could reunite the tribe by organizing a new social system. From 1736 to 1739, Prieber succeeded in winning a great deal of support among the Cherokees.

By 1740 the tribe was split into three factions: those who followed Moytoy, those who followed Prieber, and those who remained faithful to Cherokee traditions. Conditions became even more critical when some Cherokees, at Moytoy's request, joined British troops to fight against the Spanish. Their help in "King George's War" brought the Cherokees unforeseen suffering. Cherokee volunteers were issued smallpox-infested clothes and blankets. In the ensuing epidemic, hundreds of Cherokees died. Furthermore, by giving military support to the British colonists in this war, the Cherokees lost the friendship of many neighboring Indian groups.

The colonists, both French and British, were pleased with these developments. They expected the imminent collapse of the Cherokee tribe. But they waited in vain.

Cherokee Diplomacy: 1745–1759

In 1744 Attakullakulla, or Little Carpenter, the tribal peace chief who had been captured by the French, returned from captivity. He was distressed by the discord he saw, and his first requirement was the removal of "emperor" Moytoy's successor. Moytoy, killed in battle in 1741, had been replaced by his son. Such a practice was unheard of in Cherokee society, because descent was traced through the female line. Sons could never succeed their fathers in office. Little Carpenter, by persuading the emperor's followers that they were violating sacred tribal traditions, succeeded in breaking the emperor's power. Cherokee allegiances began to return to their traditional leader, the Uku.

Little Carpenter next turned to the task of reunifying the district councils. In long and frequent visits he convinced the councils to stop making separate trade arrangements with colonial administrators. He argued that the Cherokees could reassume their once profitable control over trade only if the districts began to negotiate together. Finally, Little Carpenter won over the tribal war chief, a supporter of the French, to a position of neutrality.

The British and French were aware that Little Carpenter's work had begun to revitalize the tribe. Though some discord remained in the late 1740's, the Cherokees were far more unified than they had been at the start of the decade.

The full effect of the reunification program was brought home to colonial administrators when Little Carpenter began to deal with them. He announced to colonial officials of Virginia, South Carolina, and Georgia that he had the power to cut off trade unless more favorable policies were adopted. The colonists tested his claims and realized that they were true. The governors of Virginia and South Carolina renegotiated trade agreements.

Gradually the Cherokees were regaining the upper hand. Little Carpenter traveled to neighboring Indian groups and assured them that the Cherokees were again a neutral power. He asked for their support. In most cases he obtained it.

The combination of Little Carpenter's wisdom, political skill, pride in Cherokee traditions, and diplomatic expertise created a new situation for the Cherokees by the late 1750's. The British and French settlers again competed for Cherokee trade. The tribe, largely reunified, had begun to benefit from the new harmonious conditions. Cherokee farms produced surplus crops, and trade was profitable. Although his task was not finished, Little Carpenter was a strong and effective peace chief.

Cherokee Defeat: 1759–1761

The neutrality policy of the Cherokees kept them out of the French and Indian War with the British for several years after its start in 1754. Finally, in 1759, the British colonists in Virginia persuaded the Cherokees to supply them with some men for an attack against the Shawnees. The planned attack, however, never occurred, because the expedition of British and Cherokee forces was unable to reach its intended destination.

As the group returned home, there was a fight between the Cherokees and the British. More than twenty Indians were killed. The incident touched off a series of reciprocal attacks, and peace efforts by both sides failed. The Cherokees declared allegiance with the French.

Resentful of the Cherokees' return to power, and bitter about their alliance with the French, the British colonists vowed to crush the tribe. During 1760 and 1761 hundreds of well-armed British troops attacked various Cherokee towns. With little help from their French allies, the Cherokees nevertheless successfully resisted the British for some two years. But in the summer of 1761 the British adopted a scorched-earth policy, burning Cherokee fields. Little Carpenter and the tribal Uku signed peace treaties with Virginia and South Carolina in the fall.

Though defeated, the Cherokees were not vanquished. Over the next half-century, despite the loss of most of their lands, the Cherokees rebuilt their society and prospered again. But ultimately their recovery proved as frustrating to citizens of the United States as their earlier prominence had been for the colonists. Their troubles were not over.

Cherokees and Colonial Policies

The colonists' relations with the Cherokees offer some clues to the reasons behind colonial Indian policies in general. Most colonial descriptions of the Cherokees picture them as "savages" who refused to become "civilized." In fact, as we have seen, the Cherokees had a stable and complex political system.

Colonial attacks on the Cherokees had little to do with Cherokee aggression or raids. The real reasons were probably quite different. First, the Cherokees occupied land which was increasingly coveted by the expanding colonies. Second, the Cherokees were astute traders who refused to give away their goods for less than full value. And finally, instead of being primitives who could easily be manipulated by the "civilized" colonists, the Cherokees often had the upper hand. But by claiming to be in a "kill or be killed" situation, the colonists could maintain that their own aggressive actions were justified.

Satirical figures by a modern
Indian artist: (left) starving
Indian begging for food; (right)
white bureaucrat lecturing him.

3

THE AMERICAN INDIAN
AND THE UNITED STATES
FROM 1775 TO 1870

"Go west, young man," and west he, and others, went. Within one hundred years the people who had won their independence from Great Britain extended their control from the Atlantic seaboard to the Pacific Coast. In their nation, they declared, there would be "liberty and justice for all."

But Indians were not thought to be a part of that nation, and the ideas of liberty and justice were not applied to them. At the beginning, Indian groups were regarded as "foreign and sovereign nations" by the United States. If a group of Indians were to attack Americans, they would be treated as a belligerent foreign aggressor. And so, throughout the early and middle 1800's, Indians were defeated in battles and driven from their homelands. They were ocasionally imprisoned. Most frequently, they were placed on reservations.

INDIANS AS "SOVEREIGN NATIONS"

Sporadic fighting between Amerian colonists and British troops had already begun when, in the summer of 1775, the Continental Congress took up the matter of Indian affairs. The delegates unanimously agreed on the need for better relations with what they termed "Indian nations." This phrase was the Congress' first official reference to Indian groups. It marked the beginning of an Indian policy for what was to become the United States of America.

In July 1775, the Continental Congress organized three Indian Departments to serve the North, the West, and the South. Commissioners were appointed to discourage the Indians from cooperating with the British. Their efforts were not totally successful, and several Indian groups did cooperate closely with the British during the Revolutionary War.

When peace came in 1783 and the boundaries of the United States were established, several of the Indian groups found that the territories on which they lived were claimed by the American government. These Indians were informed that because they had supported the British, they, too, would have to negotiate peace treaties or suffer the consequences.

Agents from the Indian Department informed the Indians that the new government considered each Indian group to be a separate nation. The agents then explained that their government would prefer negotiating treaties with these Indian nations to making war against them. Treaties were signed with the League of the Iroquois in 1784, with the Cherokees, Delawares, Ottawas, Chippewas, and Hurons in 1785, and with the Shawnees in 1786. Each treaty required that the Indians cede land to the new government.

Early Westward Expansion

Treaty negotiation produced very favorable results for the United States. In each treaty, certain lands were set aside for

Indian use only. The right to exclusive use of these lands was guaranteed to the Indians as long as the terms of the treaty were observed. But rarely, if ever, did the Indians actually retain lands that had been guaranteed to them. After a treaty was enacted, frontier settlers would begin to encroach on the land set aside for the Indians. The Indians, in turn, would attempt to drive off the settlers. The settlers would then demand protection from the military. With the arrival of soldiers, there was usually a battle.

The attacks on settlers and the ensuing battles between Indians and American troops were commonly regarded as Indian "uprisings." They were interpreted as proof of the untrustworthiness of the Indians. These episodes led to new treaties and further restriction of Indian land rights. This process continued until the Indians had been forced to give up claim to almost all of the land in the United States.

A typical incident occurred in Indiana Territory in 1802. The Indians of the Territory—Kickapoos, Weas, and Delawares—at first tried to resist the encroachments of the settlers. But the territorial governor, William Henry Harrison, simply told the Indians that if they did not peacefully cede their land, he would use force to make them leave.

The settlers were not the only people responsible for the breakdown of established treaties. Frequently a treaty would specify that areas inside the borders of Indian lands were to be set aside for a military fort, a trading post, a church, or a school. Because roads were necessary for easy access to such places, many of the treaties specifically authorized the clearing of roads. But the construction of roads across Indian lands encouraged the creation of even more settlements. Here the settlers were more or less innocent parties in the breakdown of treaties. The government agents who wrote the treaties authorizing these encroachments were really responsible for the subsequent upsurge in white settlement on Indian land.

Treaties were continually written and rewritten, and the Indians were dispossessed just as constantly. Many of the Indian groups became frustrated, and periodically they took matters into their own hands. After the passage of the Northwest Ordinance in 1787, Indian groups in Ohio called on British traders and soldiers for help; then they attacked American settlements. For seven years fighting continued. Finally, in 1794, the Indians lost a decisive battle with American troops and were forced to leave Ohio and eastern Indiana.

A similar situation occurred in the South. In 1785 the Creek Indians of Georgia called on the Spanish for assistance. (At this time Spain controlled Florida and the northeastern Gulf Coast.) Spain was unable to dispatch troops to help the Creeks, but it did give them weapons and other supplies. The Creeks were defeated in 1790 and were forced to sue for peace.

The Fate of Tecumseh

A significant step in the Indians' struggle for land rights was taken in the early 1800's by a Shawnee Indian named Tecumseh and his brother, the Prophet. Tecumseh maintained that Indians should unite against settlers on Indian land. Indians did not have a *title* to their land, he argued, and therefore could not sign it away. Furthermore, Tecumseh felt that land was the property of all Indians. Before any land parcel could be given away, all Indians would have to approve the transaction. For these reasons he felt that existing treaties between Indian groups and the United States were invalid.

Tecumseh visited many of the Indian groups between the Great Lakes and the Mississippi delta. He recruited volunteers willing to confront and, if necessary, to fight American forces. Considering the diversity of the groups with whom Tecumseh talked, he achieved a great deal of success.

If Tecumseh had lived at an earlier time, his plan might have worked. But in the early 1800's there were simply too many settlers west of the Appalachians. When they became uneasy and called on the United States for help, the government was quick to respond. In the winter of 1811, approximately one thousand troops led by William Henry Harrison attacked Tecumseh's headquarters on the Tippecanoe River in what is now Indiana. As historian Nelson Klose describes it, whites regarded the battle of Tippecanoe

as a great victory, since the Indians withdrew from the site when their village was burned, but more whites than Indians were killed in the battle. Harrison lost no time in sending early dispatches announcing his "victory" against the Indians. This first news caused the battle to be remembered as a decisive victory.

Tecumseh himself was not at the battle of Tippecanoe. At the time of Harrison's attack he was in the South visiting the Creek Indians, trying to secure their support. When he was told what had happened at Tippecanoe, he hurried north, reassembled his forces, and marched with them against American settlements and forts.

When the War of 1812 broke out between Great Britain and the United States, Tecumseh's forces joined the British. In October 1813, Tecumseh was killed. The movement he had brought to life rapidly disintegrated.

EARLY INDIAN POLICIES

Before the War of 1812 some of the frontier settlers, well aware of the land rights of Indians, were reluctant to enter Indian territory. This was no longer the case by the end of the war. The settlers argued that Indian support of the British during the War of 1812 had nullified Indian land rights. The settlers swarmed onto Indian territory. With the settlements came military support. Andrew Jackson led two major campaigns, against the Creeks in 1814 and against the Seminoles in 1817. Local skirmishes between the settlers and the Indians became almost routine.

Rifles, however, were only one type of weapon directed at the Indians after the War of 1812. Printer's ink was also used, and it was the press that persuaded many of the citizens of the United States that the Indian was their enemy. Books told of Indians who tortured settlers and kidnapped women and children. Some frontiersmen published their journals, many of which contained detailed descriptions of alleged Indian atrocities. In the South, where there was a great deal of concern about slavery, newspaper articles maintained that Indians, particularly the Creeks and Cherokees, were hiding escaped slaves and advocating their emancipation. The point made in all of these books and articles was that Indians were all alike—all were savages, all were heathen, none could be trusted.

Congress was forced to reevaluate its Indian policy, because the people of the United States were no longer willing to listen to arguments about Indian treaty rights. Andrew Jackson, in a letter to President Monroe, reflected the opinion of many white Americans when he wrote, "The Indians are the subjects of the United States, inhabiting its territory and acknowledging its sovereignty. Then is it not absurd for the sovereign to negotiate by treaty with the subject?"

The Drive for Indian Education

Congress refused to release all the Indian lands to public settlement for two reasons. First, the United States was deeply involved in territorial disputes with both Spain and Great Britain. Indians lived in the disputed areas. If the United States expelled the Indians and claimed their lands outright, the Indians would help Great Britain and Spain. Second, the fur trade with Indians in the West was important enough so that lawmakers did not want to risk alienating the fur-trading Indians. Congress was also aware that any action taken against Indians east of the Mississippi might well destroy the western fur trade, too, because the western Indians might sympathize with those in the East.

What the government finally did seemed at first glance to have little relation to the problem at hand. In 1819 Congress decided to appropriate $10,000 per year for the education of Indians living in Indian territory. One aspect of this educational program was instruction in the art of farming.

Why was the United States government so intent upon teaching non-farming Indians how to farm? Government officials reasoned that if all Indians could be persuaded to farm small plots of land, there would be no need for Congress to set aside huge tracts of land for Indian use. The question of releasing Indian lands to public settlement would soon become totally academic. Ultimately, the entire problem of Indian land rights would disappear.

Because the federal government lacked the organization necessary to implement such a program, the education of Indians was at first supervised by missionary societies and philanthropic groups. By 1824 at least thirty-two schools for Indians were in operation.

Indians were not receptive to the government's educational program for several reasons. First, Indian groups simply were not used to formal education. Second, schoolchildren were taken from their families every day, and the Indian parents soon became very disheartened. Third, and perhaps most important, most of the Indian groups did not want to assume "civilized" ways of life; Indians were proud of their heritage and fully satisfied with their own cultures.

The missionary societies worked valiantly to make the educational program succeed, but they failed to understand that the Indians were as attached to their own philosophies and ideas as the Christians were to theirs. The missionaries remained convinced that their efforts would be rewarded in the end. With this in mind, they discouraged immediate white settlement of the frontier. But, when they came to realize that under no circumstances would the Indians accept their ideas, the missionary societies began to support the frontiersmen. Since the Indians refused to become "civilized," in the face of the missionaries' best efforts, they would be made to suffer the consequences.

THE UPROOTING OF THE INDIANS

In 1818 Thomas McKenney, who was in charge of United States Indian policy, observed that the government needed to do one of two things: "moralize" the Indian or "exterminate" him (he favored the former). But McKenney exaggerated. There was at that time a third alternative. The United States could force the Indians living east of the Mississippi to exchange their land for territory west of the river. For some time the federal government considered such action. In 1803, after the Louisiana Purchase, Thomas Jefferson mentioned the possible advantages of transferring Indian groups to the West. By 1807 Congress had received requests from the Shawnee, Wyandot, Delaware, and Miami Indians that they be permitted to move west. Congress took no immediate action, however. During the next few years, some Cherokees moved west to an area along the Arkansas River. Congress was advised in detail about this movement.

During President Monroe's administration, John Calhoun, the Secretary of War, pressed Congress hard for the adoption of a relocation policy. Calhoun, who established the Bureau of Indian Affairs in the War Department in 1824, did not believe that treaties between the United States and Indian groups were in keeping with American interests. He agreed with Andrew Jackson, who wrote in 1820 that it was "high time to do away with the farce of treating [making treaties] with Indian tribes."

However, there was no official *removal policy*, or relocation policy, before 1828. In that year Andrew Jackson was elected President. Jackson maintained that Indians had no right to occupy land within the United States. He contended that it was only through the generosity of the United States government that Indians had any land at all. Jackson's position was supported by Congress.

The Beginnings of Indian Removal

In 1830, Congress passed the Removal Act. This act authorized surveys of land west of the Mississippi and the division of that land into districts. The land would be offered to Indian groups living east of the Mississippi, and they would be encouraged—according to the act they were not to be coerced—to exchange their lands for western territory. The act specified that Indians who chose to relocate were to be paid both for their land east of the Mississippi River and for their expenses in moving west.

But regardless of Congressional intentions, coercion did take place. The passage of the Removal Act in effect denied eastern Indian groups the protection of the federal government. Without federal protection the Indian groups were continually harassed by frontiersmen and state militias. Problems grew even worse because state legislatures were anxious to provide land for new settlers.

The Black Hawk War of 1832 grew out of these circumstances. Black Hawk was a Sauk Indian who refused to move to lands west of the Mississippi River. In 1831, with a small group of followers, he attempted to establish a farming settlement along the Illinois side of the Mississippi, on land that he claimed belonged to the Indians. Such farming settlements were permitted under the terms of a previous treaty. But the Illinois militia attacked the settlement. In 1832 Black Hawk assembled a group of about a thousand Sauks and tried to reclaim the land. During the short war that followed, all but about one hundred of his followers were slaughtered, and Black Hawk himself was captured.

Faced with such circumstances, the Indian groups east of the Mississippi River soon began to move west. Those with lands north of the Ohio River were given land in what are now the states of Iowa, Nebraska, and Kansas. Indians with land south of the Ohio River were placed in the Oklahoma area. In 1835 President Jackson reported to Congress that many of the Indian peoples had

already [been] removed and others are preparing to go, and with the exception of two small bands living in Ohio and Indiana, not exceeding 1,500 persons, and of the Cherokees, all the tribes on the east side of the Mississippi, and extending from Lake Michigan to Florida, have entered into engagements which will lead to their transplantation.

By 1840 some seventy thousand eastern Indians had been relocated west of the Mississippi.

"Indian territory" at that time consisted of all the United States land west of the Mississippi River, except for the states of Missouri and Louisiana and the Territory of Arkansas. This "Indian territory" was officially closed to American settlement first in 1830 and again in 1834. Indian groups moving into these areas were told that the land would be theirs forever. Congress reorganized the War Department's Bureau of Indian Affairs to enable federal agents to help Indian groups adjust to their new homelands. The War Department was also instructed to secure the border between the Indians and the settlers.

The promised protection was never provided. Two famous trails, the Santa Fe Trail and the Oregon Trail, cut through Indian territory. Traders, and later settlers and missionaries, made use of these trails with the government's approval. The United States now introduced conditions on its previous "guarantee."

After the Black Hawk War in 1832, settlers gained the right to live on the west side of the Mississippi River in Iowa. Five years later Congress approved settlement as far west as Iowa's Cedar River, about sixty miles west of the Mississippi. Texas became a state in 1845, and Iowa followed one year later. The Minnesota Territory was recognized in 1849, California's statehood was approved in 1850, and by the end of 1850 the Utah and New Mexico Territories were incorporated by the United States. In 1853 the Washington and Oregon Territories were formed, and in the next year Kansas and Nebraska achieved territorial status.

The United States had guaranteed that Indian land rights in the West would be upheld forever. In reality, the government's promises were broken again and again as Indians throughout the West were uprooted. The ways in which these promises were broken varied, and they should be examined separately.

Resettlement in the Great Plains

The region of the United States known as the Great Plains includes territory west of the Mississippi River and east of the Rocky Mountains, from the Canadian border to south-central Texas. The region was originally populated by Indians organized into bands and tribes. The tribes lived east of a line extending from what is now Fargo, North Dakota, to Dallas, Texas. They included the Santee (Eastern) Dakotas, Mandans, Arikaras,

Pawnees, Kansas, Osages, and Wichitas. To the west of the tribal groups lived the bands. They included the Blackfoot (Piegan) Indians of Montana, Hidatsas, Teton (Western) Dakotas, Cheyennes, Arapahos, Comanches, Kiowas, and Crows.

Some of these Indians had encountered Europeans as early as 1541. On his journey north to find the Seven Cities of Cibola, Francisco Coronado and his party of Spanish explorers traveled into what is now western Kansas. Apparently he met Wichita Indian groups there. The meeting was peaceful. French fur traders had also been active in the northern and eastern Plains in the 1600's and 1700's; the English had continued this trade after the French left. In 1804, as Lewis and Clark were traveling northward along the Missouri River, they also met peacefully with many of the Plains Indians.

After Congress passed the Removal Act in 1830, the federal government negotiated with the Osage and Kansas tribes to let the eastern Indians settle on their land. When the eastern Indians did move into the area, there were a few skirmishes, but generally the Plains Indians did not show much opposition to their presence. White settlers to the north were treated similarly. The agricultural tribes of the eastern Plains did not fight the settlers as they first began to enter Iowa and Minnesota. And early settlers in the western Plains were rarely harassed by the Indian bands there, either.

Matters changed, however, as the settlers increased in number and began to occupy land which the Indians considered especially valuable. The growing traffic on the trails to Oregon and California, the construction of military forts and of inns for travelers, and the commotion associated with the California Gold Rush of 1849 were some of the developments which prompted the once peaceful Plains Indians to begin raiding and fighting. This change in attitude was particularly true of the Indians in the western Plains.

Wanting to protect the settlers (though, according to law, it was illegal for the settlers to be in the region) and hopeful of "opening the West," the federal government forced new treaties upon the Indians. The Dakotas, both eastern and western, the Mandans, Crows, Cheyennes, and Arapahos had by 1851 agreed to cede more land to the United States. Throughout the 1850's additional treaties were signed. The discovery of gold in Colorado, and the huge influx of settlers that followed, touched off serious fighting after 1859.

In the 1830's the Choctaws, like other eastern tribes, were relocated. This detail from a painting by the Indian artist Valjean Hessing reflects the poignant mood of their trek west.

News spread among the American settlements on the Plains that the Indians were "on the warpath." Whatever friendly relations had existed between settlers and Indians broke down completely. Settlers viewed the Indian wars as a product of Indian aggression. This view is suspect, however, because the majority of Plains Indians were peace-loving people.

While the Union and Confederate forces fought the Civil War, the western settlers and the Plains Indians were involved in their own struggle. After 1865 many American troops were moved to the Plains region to help the settlers win their fight against the Indians. Battle by battle, the fight was won.

Difficulties in the Intermountain West

The Intermountain area lies between the Rocky Mountains and the Cascade and Sierra Nevada Ranges. Many anthropologists think that this area is the one into which the first Indians came and settled permanently. At one site, archeologists have found evidence of "an almost uninterrupted sequence of habitation that goes back at least 9,500 years."

The Intermountain region was settled by Indian band groups. These Indians first met Europeans when the fur traders came west. The French and English encountered Indian groups such as the Kalispels, Coeur d'Alenes, Flatheads, Spokanes, Yakimas, Wallawallas, Nez Percés, Klamaths, and Modocs. As overland routes to California were explored, American traders met the Utes and Paiutes of Utah and Nevada.

The first permanent American settlements in the Intermountain area were those established by religious groups. In 1831, a group of fur traders made their way east from Oregon with four Nez Percé Indians, who visited St. Louis and several other towns before returning home. During the course of their visit the Indians talked with William Clark, the co-leader of the Lewis and Clark expedition, who was then in charge of Indian affairs for the federal government. Clark told a missionary society that these Indians were unfamiliar with Christianity, and a group of missionaries established a settlement in Oregon in 1834.

Missionaries were responsible for the first serious outbreak of violence in the Intermountain region. In 1847, local missionaries refused to permit shamans to assist members of the Cayuse band who had contracted measles. The offended Cayuses retaliated. Fourteen white Americans were killed in the ensuing fighting. White Americans by that time had settled throughout the Intermountain region. After this incident they began to regard the Indians in Oregon and Washington with suspicion and distrust. The recent appearance of miners and loggers made the situation even more tense.

Conditions were somewhat more peaceful to the south. The Mormon settlers of Utah did manage to coexist with local Indians. Other settlers of the area, however, were far more aggressive than the Mormons. Violence came belatedly to Utah, but it arrived nevertheless.

In the mid-1850's, a number of treaties were made requiring the Intermountain Indians to cede land. The usual guarantee, that is, "this land will be yours forever," was made in every case. But the "guaranteed" land rights were usually ignored within a few years after the treaties were signed. The Washos and Paiutes in Nevada retained a certain amount of independence, simply because Americans were not interested in settling in their arid homeland until the late 1800's.

The Uprooting of the Pacific Coast Indians

The Pacific Coast region was heavily populated by Indians. In the north, nonagricultural chiefdoms exchanged fish, vegetable foods, and game. Farther south there were tribes, and throughout the entire area hunting and gathering bands were common.

The first whites to contact the Pacific Coast groups were seagoing explorers. Spaniards and Russians arrived by ship and traded with the Indians. A Franciscan mission was established in San Diego as early as 1769. Relations between Indians and whites in this early period were quite peaceful.

Overland expeditions to California occurred as early as 1826. Explorers for the American Fur Company reached the Oregon and Washington coasts even earlier. A few settlers managed to stay in California during the 1830's (then under Mexican control). And by 1841 a group of settlers had reached the San Joaquin Valley.

The Pacific Coast Indians were numerous and diverse. Even so, they had lived in this region for centuries without fighting. The Indians who met the early explorers were friendly and often traded with them. When the Spanish came into the area to establish missions, they did not encounter trouble.

The Franciscan missionaries who arrived on the Pacific Coast were originally friendly toward the Indians there. The soldiers who accompanied the missionaries, however, antagonized the Indians by forcing them to live in mission communities. By the time settlers reached the Pacific Coast, many of the Indian groups had become hostile toward all newcomers. Serious difficulties, however, did not appear until 1849, a year after gold was discovered in California. A group of "Forty-Niners" attacked Indians whom they referred to as "Diggers"—so-called because of their method of searching for edible roots. Ray A. Billington describes the assault in his book *Westward Expansion:*

The miners fell upon them with savage fury, driving them from their homes, murdering their warriors, and using every feeble attempt at retaliation as an excuse to exterminate whole tribes. When the federal government belatedly intervened, only a handful [out of an estimated population of 150,000] of "Diggers" remained to be herded into reservations.

When California was admitted as a state in 1850, the government forced the Indians to relinquish their land. Treaties to this end were quickly signed, but often only after the Indians occupying the land had already been attacked. As had happened to Indians along the eastern seaboard when the colonists arrived there, the Pacific Coast Indians were also displaced. On new land in the interior, the Indians who had been used to coastal life had to adapt to a new environment. A number of Indian groups were unable to adapt, and sometimes entire groups simply disappeared. Those that did survive were often harassed by settlers. The Quinault, Tillamook, Yurok, Shasta, Miwok, and Yokuts groups were a few of the Indians who lost their lands and lives when the Pacific Coast was settled.

Violence in the Southwest

The Southwest includes southern Utah and Colorado and the states of Arizona and New Mexico. It was in this region that farming was first developed by North American Indians. The Hohokams, who lived in southern Arizona, farmed with irrigation canals as early as two thousand years ago. When Europeans made contact with the Indians of the Southwest through Spanish exploration in 1538 and 1540, they met the Papagos and Pimas, and they visited the villages of the Zuñis, Hopis, Acomas, and others. When the Spanish colonized New Mexico in 1598, they came to know many other Pueblo groups and the Apaches.

American settlers first met the Indians of the Southwest in the 1820's, on the Santa Fe Trail. Spanish and Mexican settlers told the Americans that the southwestern Indians—the Apaches, Navajos, Havasupais, Walapais, and Yavapais—were extremely hostile and dangerous warriers. Many writers have also referred to the aggressiveness of these Indians, and some have even written that they were instinctive warriors.

In fact, the southwestern Indians were no more aggressive than any other Indians in North America. Coronado's battles with these Indians were started by the actions of his own men. The so-called Pueblo War of 1680 was the result of almost a century of Spanish cruelty to the village Indians along the Rio Grande. Raiding by the Navajos and the Apaches was prompted by white settlement of lands which these Indians had traditionally used for hunting.

Prior to 1846 the Southwest was controlled first by the Spanish and later by the Mexicans. The United States came to control it through the settlement of the Mexican War in 1848 and the Gadsden Purchase of 1853.

Gold along the Gila River lured the first significant number of American settlers to the Southwest; cattle raising later brought additional permanent settlers. After three hundred years of experience with the Spanish and the Mexicans, the Indians were suspicious of settlers. They were reluctant to let the newcomers settle in their homeland. Colonel Stephen Kearny and other military men signed treaties with the various groups. The Indians had no more intention of observing their treaty terms than did the American settlers. By the 1860's the Southwest was the scene of constant skirmishes and fighting. The American government sometimes even persuaded certain Indian groups to fight alongside the United States cavalry against other Indians in the area.

Other farming tribes, such as the villagers along the Rio Grande, did not violently oppose the settlers. These villagers, the Pueblo Indians, had been in contact with Spanish and Mexican colonists for several centuries. Because of this contact they had adopted many elements of the culture of the whites. For example, they had churches in or near many of their villages. Their people wore "Western style" clothes. Each village had its own administrative officers. When the first settlers from the United States met the Pueblos, they immediately regarded these Indians as civilized. Such occurrences, however, were rare in the Southwest.

Throughout the Southwest, settlers moved in and occupied Indian land. Treaties were signed and forgotten; new treaties were negotiated. Indians in the Southwest were eventually confined to canyons and deserts where hunting, fishing, and farming were almost impossible. The record of settlement in the Southwest is the same as the record elsewhere—a nearly total disregard by the settlers for the rights of the Indians.

CONQUEST AND DEPENDENCE

The earliest leaders of the American nation were cautious in their dealings with Indians. As the United States grew in strength and power, this caution was replaced by disregard for the Indians' welfare. In the beginning, as you recall, the United States regarded Indian groups as "sovereign nations." Nearly a hundred years later, in 1871, Congress passed the following resolution:

Hereafter no Indian nation or tribe within the territory of the United States shall be acknowledged or recognized as an independent tribe or power with whom the United States may contract by treaty.

Fifty-one years after Andrew Jackson had denounced treaty making as a "farce," Congress turned his opinion into law.

In the period that followed the passage of the Removal Act, American policy toward the Indians became much less diplomatic. The case of the Cherokees is an example. In 1827 the Cherokees had adopted a constitutional form of government. They maintained that they were a sovereign nation and, as such, were due respect befitting this status.

The land on which the Cherokees lived was also claimed by the state of Georgia. Georgia asserted in 1828 that it had the right to demand allegiance from Indians as well as non-Indians living within its borders and, in addition, to expel any person or group that did not recognize Georgia's sovereignty. The Cherokee "nation" thereupon sued the state of Georgia. In 1832, two years after the passage of the Removal Act, the Supreme Court ruled that the state of Georgia did not have the right to extend its laws over the Cherokee nation. President Jackson is reported to have responded, "[Chief Justice] John Marshall has made his decision: now let him enforce it."

Marshall's decision was never enforced. The relocation of the Cherokees, according to the terms of the Removal Act, was to be voluntary. But the Cherokees did not wish to move west. After a long series of arguments, bribes, threats, and tricks, a treaty between the United States and the Cherokee nation was signed, and the Cherokees were finally uprooted; their terrible westward trek has become known as the "Trail of Tears." A federal government document, published in 1900, contains the following description:

... troops were disposed at various points throughout the Cherokee country, where stockade forts were erected for gathering in and holding the Indians preparatory to removal. From these, squads of troops were sent to search out with rifle and bayonet every small cabin hidden away in the coves or by the sides of mountain streams, to seize and bring in as prisoners all the occupants, however or wherever they might be found. . . . A Georgia volunteer, afterward a colonel in the Confederate service, said: "I fought through the civil war and have seen men shot to pieces and slaughtered by thousands, but the Cherokee removal was the cruelest I ever knew."

The Cherokee expulsion was approved by Congress in 1838. President Jackson had left the White House two years earlier. Apparently other Americans agreed with Jackson that the United States should become more aggressive in its dealings with the Indians.

The Removal Act provided for the appointment of Indian agents to serve in Indian territory and to administer policy at the local level. Until 1849 the Bureau of Indian Affairs was under the direction of the Secretary of War. The Indian Department was a branch of the War Department because in the early years of the American republic the Indian "problem" was mainly one of persuading Indians to remain neutral in the event of an American war with Great Britain and Spain. Through the years, however, the Indian Department became closely identified with the military campaigns against Indian groups. The department's Indian agents, in fact, were sometimes the ones who instigated skirmishes between Indian groups and American military forces.

The "Winning" of the West

In 1849 Congress transferred the Bureau of Indian Affairs to the newly formed Department of the Interior. This action was the result of concern over land policy, not Indian welfare. The Pre-emption Act of 1841 and the "opening of the West" required the federal government to. meet the problem of land use. The two government agencies, working together, coerced Indians to agree to treaties that provided them with the most undesirable and barren land in America. Dozens of such treaties were signed and processed within a few years. The land-use decisions of the Interior Department were favorable to the settlers. Indian groups often complained bitterly to agents of the Bureau of Indian Affairs, but because the Bureau was responsible to the Interior Department, their complaints were generally ignored.

In 1861, treaty plans were presented to the Cheyennes and Arapahos. These peoples were to be restricted to a small parcel of land between the Arkansas River and Sand Creek in eastern Colorado. Dissatisfied with the treaty, both groups refused to remain in the region set aside for their use. For the next three years, they attempted to negotiate, then pleaded, and finally turned to violence in despair.

By 1864 it seemed that the Cheyennes and Arapahos had won their fight; settlers in western Nebraska and eastern Colorado were offering little resistance. The Cheyenne leader, Black Kettle, went to the governor of the Colorado Territory to announce that the Cheyennes and Arapahos were now satisfied and would fight no longer. A month after this meeting, Black Kettle conveyed the same message to the federal military commander at Fort Lyon.

The governor of Colorado, however, would not accept what he interpreted as an Indian victory. In November 1864, following the governor's orders, nearly a thousand soldiers and militiamen attacked Black Kettle's encampment along Sand Creek. Most of the warriors were several miles away hunting buffalo, and two thirds of the Indians who remained in the undefended camp were women and children. When the troops charged, at dawn, Black Kettle displayed an American flag as a symbol of friendship. It had no effect. By midday over a hundred Indians—mostly women and children—had been killed and mutilated. The toll of this encounter, the Sand Creek Massacre, would have been even higher if the attackers had not been confused and disorganized.

During the middle and late 1860's there was further bloody fighting on the Plains. Nearly every group of Plains Indians, from the Mandans in the north to the Kiowas in the south, was involved at one time or another. In 1867 Congress passed a bill to encourage peace with the Indians then at war with the United States.

The bill provided for the establishment of reservations for Indian groups and for the appointment of a Peace Commission to determine their location.

The peace commissioners decided that the Black Hills in South Dakota would be used as a reservation for the northern Plains Indians, while the area that is now the state of Oklahoma would be reserved for the southern Plains groups. Both of these proposals met with the approval of the Interior Department, and, with military assistance, the treaties of Medicine Lodge (Oklahoma) and Fort Laramie (Black Hills) were signed. While the western Plains bands were being relocated, the farming tribes in the East were also being forced to accept reassignment. By 1866, most of the remaining Cherokees, Chickasaws, Choctaws, and other groups were all transferred to Oklahoma.

The same type of procedure was followed in the Southwest. Beginning in 1864, the Mescalero Apaches and the Navajos were taken captive by forces under Colonel Kit Carson. They were then transferred to Fort Sumner in New Mexico. The Navajos were forced to march about three hundred miles to get there. The barren reservation at Fort Sumner, called the Bosque Redondo, was a failure in every respect. In 1868, the Navajos were transferred to a new reservation in northern Arizona.

In the Intermountain area, Indians were also assigned to reservations, and by 1870 the Pacific Coast area was spotted with a number of small reservations as well.

THE INDIANS AS SUBJECT PEOPLES

The reservation system did not work as planned. The government was unable to prevent settlers from violating the boundaries of the reservations. Fighting again broke out in the Plains in 1869. The Indians were once more blamed for not having observed the terms of the treaties.

Pressure from special interest groups was a chief reason that Congress decided, in 1871, to disallow any future treaty negotiation with Indian groups. The pressure came from railroad magnates, ranchers, state legislatures interested in the settlement of land, and persons concerned about the costs of treaties (treaties had come to involve the payment of sums of money in exchange for land). All these groups were upset that the reservation system had not solved their problems. As Congress debated the Appropriations Bill of 1871, many of the Senators, pressured by these special interest groups, argued against providing funds for future treaties. One Senator, the chairman of the Senate Committee on Indian Affairs, stated: "I have been of the impression for years that there was no necessity for negotiating and ratifying treaties with Indians; that all our intercourse with them could be regulated by law, by statutory provisions, just as well as by treaty." The Appropriations Bill was revised. After 1871, no more treaties were made between the United States and Indian groups.

With the passage of the Appropriations Bill of 1871, the Indians became subjects of the United States without their consent. It should be stressed that the Indians were subjects, not citizens. Congress did not grant citizenship to Indians until 1924, fifty-three years later. In other words, although the Indians were required to obey the laws of the United States, they could not elect representatives to help govern them. Although the Indians were now an official part of the nation, they were to have no voice in its destiny. It should be remembered that one of the reasons given by the authors of the Declaration of Independence for their revolt against Great Britain had been that they and their countrymen were "subject . . . to a jurisdiction foreign [to them] and unacknowledged by [their] laws."

In 1871 the conquest of the Indians was in almost every respect complete. Once sovereign nations, the Indians had become subject peoples. A Senator who recognized the issues in the 1871 debate observed:

I know what the misfortune of the tribes is. Their misfortune is not that they are red men; not that they are semi-civilized, not that they are a dwindling race, not that they are a weak race. Their misfortune is that they hold great bodies of rich lands, which have aroused the cupidity of powerful corporations and of powerful individuals. . . . I greatly fear that the adoption of this provision to discontinue treaty-making . . . is the first step in a great scheme of spoliation, in which the Indians will be plundered, corporations and individuals enriched, and the American name dishonored in history.

SUGGESTED FURTHER READING

Jackson, Helen Hunt, A Century of Dishonor: The Early Crusade for Indian Reform, ed. by Andrew F. Rolle. New York: Harper & Row, 1965.

Josephy, Alvin M., Jr., *The Indian Heritage of America.* New York: Alfred A. Knopf, 1968.

Pearce, Roy H., *The Savages of America.* Baltimore: Johns Hopkins Press, 1965.

Prucha, Francis P., *American Indian Policy in the Formative Years.* Cambridge, Mass.: Harvard University Press, 1962.

Spicer, Edward H., *Cycles of Conquest.* Tucson, Arizona: University of Arizona Press, 1962.

a case study:

THE CONQUEST
OF THE NEZ PERCÉS

On October 5, 1877, after valiantly trying to defend their rights, the Nez Percé Indians were forced into surrender by the United States Army. These people were one of the last Indian groups to be conquered. They offer a vivid example of the effects of Indian policy in the first century of United States history.

Nez Percé Society

The Nez Percés occupied a vast territory in the Intermountain region. The area covered lands in western Idaho, southeastern Washington, and northeastern Oregon.

The Nez Percés were a stable society long before Europeans came to North America. Their people were organized into small, independent band groups. Each band had its own particular economic practices. Fishing was important to those who lived near lakes or streams. Groups in the mountains hunted game. Some bands moved seasonally from valleys to mountains, in order to harvest the different wild plants that grew in these places.

Trading was important to the Nez Percés. Various bands exchanged goods among themselves, and some of them traded with neighboring peoples. Trade brought the Nez Percés into regular contact with Indians along the Pacific Coast and in the western Plains.

In the early 1700's the Nez Percés acquired horses from the Plains Indians. This was a significant development, because it allowed them to expand their trade routes in all directions. Soon the Nez Percés heard of white men from other Indians. The Nez Percés were curious about these men, with their interest in furs and their unusual trade goods. Some of the Nez Percé bands anxiously awaited a chance to make contact with the whites.

The Nez Percés and the Fur Trade

When Lewis and Clark arrived in Nez Percé country in September 1805, they were given a warm and cordial welcome. Clark wrote that not only was his party provided with food and gifts, but a Nez Percé man also gave them a detailed description of the region. Perhaps the Indian was trying to impress Clark with trade possibilities.

By that time some of the Nez Percé bands had already plunged deeply into the fur trade. Some bands were supplying pelts to traders from a British Canadian firm, the North West Company. Other Nez Percé traders returned from the Dakotas with rifles received in exchange for furs. After 1805 the fur trade boomed.

While the fur trade had posed problems for many other Indian groups, it was beneficial for the Nez Percés. To them, trading was an honored tradition. It supplied them not only with needed goods, but also with important information about other societies.

During thirty years of fur trading the Nez Percés learned a great deal about white society. Many learned how to use the languages of the Canadian and American traders. When the traders discussed the War of 1812, the Nez Percés learned about white men's nations and warfare. They probably first heard about American wars with Indians and about American Indian policy from the traders. The Nez Percés became increasingly familiar with the attitudes and business practices of white society.

Whenever they had the chance, the Nez Percés tried to learn more about the whites. With assistance from the Hudson's Bay Company they sent some of their children to a mission school in central Canada. And in 1831, as you have already read, they sent four of their men to St. Louis with a group of traders.

The Arrival of Missionaries and Settlers

Protestant missionaries first arrived in the Northwest in 1834. The Nez Percés noted their arrival with keen interest. There had been a severe decline in the fur trade, and the Nez Percés hoped that missionaries could help them develop new trade markets. Thus they encouraged missionaries to come to their territory. In 1836, the Reverend Henry Spalding and his wife Eliza responded. They erected a church and school near the present site of Lewiston, Idaho.

The Nez Percés wasted no time. They told the Spaldings they wanted to learn how to read and write English. They wanted the missionaries to teach them about American society and American ideas. In this way they learned of plans to bring American settlers to the Northwest. The news was exciting—the arrival of settlers meant a new trade market!

Preparations began immediately. Few of the Nez Percés knew about farming, but they did know that the settlers would need grain and vegetables when they arrived. Therefore, some of the Nez Percé group asked the Spaldings to teach them how to farm. Others learned how to care for livestock, so that they would have meat and milk to offer.

When the settlers arrived, the Nez Percés had food and livestock to offer them in trade. The Indians drove hard bargains, but the weary and hungry settlers were happy to deal with them.

The Nez Percés wanted the missionaries to live on their land only as long as they were useful. Then they told them to leave. Several missionaries were permitted to stay only a year or two. The Spaldings themselves were eventually told to leave.

The Nez Percés and the American Government

During the fur-trading period only a few Nez Percé groups were actually involved in trading activities. Similarly, only a few of them farmed or raised livestock during the missionary period. Diversity was basic to Nez Percé society. These people were not a "tribe" or a "nation." They were a loose association of independent groups. Each group had its own leaders; there was no single leader who could speak for all of them.

This sort of organization, in which all people were considered equal in authority and responsibility, had served the Nez Percés successfully for generations. It was precisely the looseness of this organization, however, that led to their downfall under American domination.

The first official meeting between the Nez Percés and a representative of the American government was arranged by the Spaldings in 1842. The

Indians thought the meeting was intended for an exchange of information. A large group of Nez Percé people, representing a number of local bands, were present. They were eager to find out about the American government and its plans; they hoped, in turn, to be able to tell the new Indian agent something about themselves.

They were quickly disappointed. The agent, Elijah White, was not interested in their ideas or their organization. He announced that one of their old men, a person the Americans called Ellis, was to be their "head chief" and that they were to appoint twelve other men as "subchiefs" to represent them on a council. White then read them a "Code of Laws." Unless these were followed, he said, the people would be punished.

Generally, the Nez Percés were able to ignore White and his code of laws. Most of them lived far enough away from American settlements so as not to be bothered. White did put pressure on those who lived close to the mission, but the Spaldings eased things as much as they could.

White left the region in 1845, and two years later the Nez Percés told the Spaldings to leave. The Indians were free from American interference for a few years. During this time they discussed what they would do if, and when, American administrators returned. They knew that other Indian groups had tried to fight the Americans and had been conquered. They agreed that this approach was worthless.

The Indians decided the best approach would be to work out a peaceful arrangement with the Americans. The different bands would continue to act separately. If the Americans wanted a man named as "head chief," the Nez Percés would consent, but only for the sake of negotiations. The "head chief" was not to be considered a man of any kind of power.

In 1853 Governor Isaac Stevens of Washington Territory began to arrange treaties with the Indians. As the Nez Percés had expected, the Americans asked them to name a leader. They named a man who was called Lawyer.

In 1855, the Nez Percés signed a treaty with the Americans at Walla Walla. They returned satisfied that their strategy had worked. Though they had ceded some of their lands to the Americans, they retained the land that they regarded as the most valuable. Soon they were again busy with their normal activities. Bands hunted and fished without interference. Farmlands produced high yields. Trade continued to be profitable.

Suddenly, in 1860, the discovery of gold on Nez Percé lands put an end to this period of peace. Hordes of whites, with no regard for past treaties, streamed into the territory. Nez Percé farms and homes were overrun. Hunting grounds were ruined. Individual Nez Percés were killed.

Nez Percé representatives appealed to the American government for help. They pointed out that they had kept the terms of the treaty of 1855. Now the Americans must do the same.

Some ineffective efforts were made by the American government. But the miners continued to upset Nez Percé life. Then, in 1863, federal commissioners arrived and suggested that the Nez Percés could be better protected if they ceded additional territory.

The Nez Percés, understandably, were at first unanimously opposed to this idea. However, Lawyer and some other leaders finally gave in. They agreed to live on the small Lapwai Reservation in Idaho. Those who refused to go were told that they could no longer expect American protection. But by that time, the gold fever had ebbed. The remaining Nez Percés returned to their lands, where they again lived peacefully.

The Surrender of the Nez Percés

The final crisis for the Nez Percés grew out of further demands by settlers for land in Nez Percé territory. Settlers began to move onto lands still held by the Nez Percé groups who had refused to move to the reservation in 1863. The Indians insisted that the settlers had no right to this territory, because it had been guaranteed to the Indians by the 1855 treaty. Their appeal was honored by President Grant. In 1873, he ordered the settlers to leave. But the governor of Oregon defended the settlers, and two years later Congress reversed the President's decision.

The Indians continued to appeal, but in vain. Government administrators met with the remaining Nez Percé groups and threatened to use force unless the Indians agreed to join the rest of their people on the Lapwai Reservation. Reluctantly, the remaining Nez Percés submitted, agreeing to move by the summer of 1877.

Thus, when summer came, several hundred Nez Percés began a trek over the mountains from Oregon into Idaho in compliance with the federal decision. The groups stopped for ceremonial purposes at the border of the Lapwai Reservation. It was an emotional occasion. They realized they were saying goodbye to a way of life they had followed for generations; they looked for strength to adjust to the new requirements. Nerves were taut.

During the ceremonial period a tragedy occurred. The exact nature of the incident that started it is still disputed. A group of young Nez Percé horsemen charged into nearby white settlements, terrorizing the residents and killing several whites. But according to the Nez Percés, these raids were in retaliation for the cold-blooded murder of two elderly Indians by white miners a day or so before. Whatever their cause, the raids brought a retaliatory attack on the Nez Percé encampment by American forces stationed nearby.

The Nez Percés had never been involved in a war against American forces. Even at this point they were not interested in war. Hastily, the leaders gathered and decided to get their people completely out of the area. They left the campsite immediately and hid in the surrounding hills. As soon as possible, they would depart for new land in the Plains.

The government was determined to put the Nez Percés on the Lapwai Reservation. Soldiers tried to force them to come out of the hills and surrender. A bloody battle was fought, but the Nez Percés escaped capture. They began to travel eastward. For two months, and in spite of several skirmishes, the Indians successfully eluded American troops.

The group reached the area of the present-day Yellowstone Park, in Wyoming. There the leaders took stock of the situation. They could not be free in the Plains, where Indians had already been captured and placed on reservations. Their people were tired, hungry, and unable to fight much longer. They decided to head for Canada, where other Indians had found new homelands.

The group turned north. They had almost reached the Canadian border when they were cut off by American troops sent from the east. For five days the Nez Percés fought desperately. But they were tired from the long march. The skirmishes along the way had taken their toll, and many of their fighters were dead.

Finally, on October 5, 1877, a Nez Percé leader called Chief Joseph rode into the American encampment to surrender. Joseph told the American commander, "I am tired of fighting. Our chiefs are killed. . . . It is cold and we have no blankets. The little children are freezing to death. . . . my heart is sick and sad. From where the sun now stands, I will fight no more forever."

The Nez Percés in Captivity

Joseph and his people were shipped to exile on a reservation in Oklahoma, far from their homelands in the Northwest. There many died, their spirits broken. Others were killed in epidemics that were intensified by polluted water, overcrowded living conditions, and inadequate food.

Eventually, Joseph's people were moved back to the Northwest. But not to the Lapwai Reservation, where the other Nez Percés lived. Instead, they were assigned to the Colville Reservation in Washington. There they were near, but not close enough to be with, their relatives and friends on the Idaho reservation.

Peyote rite, detail
from a painting by
the Indian artist
Al Momaday

4

THE AMERICAN INDIAN
AND THE UNITED STATES
AFTER 1870

In the second century of its relations with the Indian people, the United States gradually replaced the battlefield with the classroom, the rifle with the schoolbook, and the soldier with the teacher. In these ways the American government hoped to show Indians the benefits of Western civilization.

The alleged savagery of the Indians had been a matter of concern for the United States from the very beginning. Even before 1870 some missionary groups in the United States had tried to "civilize" the "savages." Generally, however, the missionaries' efforts had met with failure.

By 1870 the situation had changed. By then most of the Indians had been conquered and confined to reservations. The Indians were now a defenseless, captive audience. White Americans were convinced that by teaching them English, Christianity, and the principle of working for wages they could convince the Indians to give up their old customs and accept the "American" way of life.

Government officials were confident they would succeed. Schools and churches were constructed on the reservations, and teachers and missionaries were recruited to work with the Indians. But to the surprise of many, the expected results were not achieved. By the 1970's, after a full century of efforts to educate, Christianize, and persuade the Indians to work for wages, the American government could claim few positive results. Indian educational achievement was far below the national norm. Only a small minority of Indians were members of Christian churches, and the use of Indian languages had continued on reservations throughout the nation. The Indians had managed to preserve their cultural identity in the face of immense pressures.

CIVILIZATION AND CHRISTIANIZATION

The first steps toward a new Indian policy had been taken in 1867. At that time, as you recall, Congress appointed a Peace Commission to negotiate reservation treaties. The Peace Commission also was to provide federal services for Indians on the reservations. These services included the provision of emergency food rations, housing materials, agricultural supplies, and educational instruction. The services were to be supplied by federal Indian agents permanently stationed on the reservations.

More drastic changes in Indian policy, however, were made in 1869. In April of that year Congress authorized President Grant to appoint a *Board of Indian Commissioners*. The commissioners were to examine federal Indian policy and make recommendations for its improvement. Because the Board's recommendations were so influential, it is worthwhile to look at some of the circumstances behind its decisions.

After the close of the Civil War in 1865, many Americans were deeply concerned about the state of the nation. They hoped to identify and correct the problems that had led to the war. Some saw immoral behavior and a lack of attention to Christian practices as two of the main problems. This conviction was publicized in churches, newspapers, and books. Within a few years many parts of the country witnessed a religious revival.

At about the same time other kinds of reform movements began to prosper. One of these stressed the need to replace the spoils system, in which politicians appointed their friends to government jobs, with an employment system based on merit. Another significant reform movement demanded more and better public education facilities.

These three developments—religious revivalism, agitation for civil service reform, and concern for educational improvements—played a role in the recommendations of the Board of Indian Commissioners. The Board suggested that Protestant church groups should be given exclusive control over the administration of Indian reservations. They argued that Indian agents should be appointed by church groups and not through the spoils system, and that Indians should be instructed by teachers appointed by the churches. In 1870 Congress approved these recommendations. The program became known either as the Peace Policy or *Civilization and Christianization.*

The new program was designed to correct existing problems. However, it immediately created different ones. The Board had recommended that exclusive administrative powers be given to specific church groups. The intention was to permit these groups to work without interference or interruption. It was hoped they would thus be better able to perform their tasks. The churches' administrative powers, however, did not necessarily insure the cooperation of the Indians. Schools and churches were built; worship services and class sessions were scheduled. But many of the Indians saw no reason to attend classes and church services.

Faced with this type of Indian apathy, the church groups on the reservations tried various methods of persuasion. Force was the most effective and common method. Missionaries and soldiers went to Indian homes and, in many cases, literally carried children to school against the wishes of their parents. The missionaries also made religious instruction and worship a requirement for receiving federal services.

Growing Indian Resistance

The use of force by the missionaries intensified resistance by the Indians. Indian parents hid their children from the missionaries and soldiers who came to take the children to school. Children who were taken to school often ran away at the earliest opportunity. In some cases resentful Indians burned the school buildings. Individual missionaries were occasionally captured and held hostage by Indian parents until their children were returned. When federal agents withheld government services from Indians who refused to attend church, the Indians sometimes destroyed the government warehouses on the reservations or the farms upon which the missionaries depended. Frequently the Indians left the reservation and raided frontier settlements to obtain food and supplies which the missionaries refused to provide. Sometimes they simply ran away.

The church groups became extremely upset over these developments. The reports they submitted to the Board of Indian Commissioners related the ways in which the Indians had rejected their overtures. Congress responded dramatically. The Appropriations Bill of 1871, mentioned in Chapter 3, was in part a response to pressure from these religious leaders. This bill, as you recall, changed the status of Indian groups from sovereign nations to subjects.

In 1872 the Commissioner of Indian Affairs told Congress that

the Indians should be made as comfortable on, and as uncomfortable off, their reservations as it was in the power of the Government to make them. . . . [It is] essential that the right of the Government to keep Indians upon the reservations assigned to them, and to arrest and return them whenever they wander away, should be placed beyond dispute.

Congress maintained that such regulations already existed. In effect, Congress gave sanction to the arbitrary arrest and imprisonment of Indians.

That same year Congress reaffirmed the exclusive administrative rights of the churches. Such reaffirmations were made periodically until 1880. The end result was the denial of religious freedom to Indians. Depending on their reservation, Indians were expected to become either Presbyterians, Methodists, members of the Christian Reformed Church, or members of another denomination. If they refused, they were to be completely deprived of federal services.

After several years of Civilization and Christianization, fighting between Indians and the United States broke out once more. In the Intermountain region Bannock and Ute groups, as well as the Nez Percés, battled American troops. In the Southwest the Apaches refused to submit to confinement on reservations. They also struggled, and they ingeniously maintained their independence for years.

The Battle of the Little Bighorn

Some of the reasons why Civilization and Christianization failed are illustrated by events in the Black Hills area in Dakota Territory. In 1868 a treaty had confined different groups of Sioux and Northern Cheyenne Indians to this area. The treaty clearly stipulated that the land was reserved solely for Indian use, and that outsiders were banned from the territory.

When the treaty's terms were announced, local settlers objected strongly. They maintained that the land was far too valuable to be given to Indians. Rumors that there was gold in the region focused further attention on the Black Hills. Mining companies and land speculators wanted the reservation lands opened for purchase and settlement. Demands were made on Congress to retract or revise the treaties.

In the summer of 1874, the army sent an expedition under Colonel George Armstrong Custer to reconnoiter the area. In August, after a two-month survey, Custer reported the discovery of gold. Although this claim was immediately denied by an expedition geologist, the local settlers listened only to Custer. "Gold fever" spread quickly, and miners began crossing the reservation borders.

Skeptical of Custer's report, Congress authorized a second expedition the next summer. Again, scientists accompanying the troops found no significant deposits of gold. However, demands for a change in the treaties did not decrease.

In the fall of 1875, federal officials met with the Indian leaders to see if the Indians would sell the land. They refused. The land had been legally assigned to them, and their people needed every square foot of it.

Several weeks after this meeting, in December, federal officials ordered all the Indians in the territory to report to reservation agencies by February 1, 1876; any Indians who did not do so would be rounded up by the army. Some of the Indians complied, but many resisted, regarding the order as another case of government treachery. Others were simply unable to reach the reservation agencies through midwinter snows.

The army assigned General Philip Sheridan to capture the Indians who disobeyed the federal orders. Sheridan's plan was to have troops enter the reservation from the east, south, and west. But by this time the Indians were prepared to fight. On June 17, 1876, a group led by Crazy Horse stopped General George Crook's advance from the south. At about the same time, the commander of the forces moving in from the east authorized Colonel Custer and Major Marcus Reno to attack the encampment of Sioux and Northern Cheyennes along the Little Bighorn River.

The Battle of the Little Bighorn took place on June 25, 1876. It was a major defeat for the United States Army and a great victory for the Indians. Custer and his entire party, and most of Reno's, were killed by Indian forces led by Crazy Horse, Gall, and Sitting Bull.

Although the Indians won some significant battles, eventually they lost the fight. By the end of 1876 most of the Sioux and Northern Cheyennes were captured and assigned to new, and smaller, reservations. The Black Hills were opened to settlement. News of the events, however, had spread. Many United States citizens were enraged at the way in which the Indians had been treated. Sitting Bull, who had successfully escaped to Canada with a small group of Sioux, was regarded as a hero by many people, Indians and non-Indians alike. Public pressures on Congress began to demand a change in Indian policy.

CREATION OF THE BOARDING SCHOOLS

By the late 1870's reservation church groups and the Board of Indian Commissioners began to reconsider Indian policy. There had been few tangible results, in spite of much hard work. After some deliberation, the Board recommended three major changes to Congress: first, that Congress take the administration of the reservations out of the hands of the church groups; second, that Congress revoke the exclusive rights (such as the power to appoint teachers) that each church group enjoyed; and third, that Congress provide funds to build and operate Indian boarding schools. These boarding schools were to be built at great distances from the reservations.

This last recommendation stemmed from the idea that full attention had to be given to the children if Civilization and Christianization were to be successful. The Board felt that adult Indians were too attached to their old customs to accept change. But the children, if removed from reservation surroundings, would probably be more receptive to different ideas. If all went according to the Board's plan, Indian culture would be effectively destroyed.

These ideas were reinforced by an experiment conducted by a military officer, Captain Richard Pratt. In 1875 he was placed in charge of a group of young Indian prisoners sent to St. Augustine, Florida, from the Great Plains region. Pratt decided to offer the prisoners industrial training during their confinement. By early 1878, when it came time to return the Indians to their reservations, many of them actually wanted to remain in the East and continue their education. Later the same year the government gave Pratt permission to try a similar experiment with a group of Sioux.

Pratt's success created a great deal of interest and enthusiasm, and Congress soon adopted the three recommendations of the Board of Indian Commissioners. However, the new boarding schools were to be run by various Protestant churches.

In 1879 Pratt was given permission to use a vacated army post at Carlisle, Pennsylvania, for an Indian boarding school. It was to be run under the auspices of the Presbyterian church. At the end of the year Pratt reported that he had enrolled 158 students at Carlisle. With the encouragement of the Board of Indian Commissioners, Congress rapidly approved funds for the construction of more Indian boarding schools. During the 1880's a number of schools were organized in different parts of the country. Congressional action was reinforced by reports like one made by Pratt in which he disclosed that children at the boarding schools were in fact "hostages for [the] good behavior of parents" on the reservations.

Life at the Boarding Schools

The boarding school environment was based on the conviction that Indian traditions were useless. The Indian Bureau directed its agents to take Indian children from their parents "first by persuasion; if this fails, then by withholding rations or annuities or by other such means as may reach the desired end." In other words, it made no difference whether the parents agreed or not to part with their children.

At the boarding schools, children were forbidden to use any language but English. If they did not know how to speak English, they had to remain silent until they learned. They had to attend classes and worship services conducted by missionary teachers. They were given food and clothing, but the clothing was often flimsy or ragged, and the diet was generally lacking in fruits, vegetables, and dairy products. The children were also required to do heavy work on the schools' farms and in their laundries, boiler rooms, and offices. The children were not permitted to return to their families until they had completed their schooling, even if this took several years. During vacations the children either remained at the school or were taken home by missionary families or other volunteers.

As far as the federal government was concerned, the boarding school program was an unqualified success. During the 1880's Congress approved funds for the construction of additional boarding schools on the reservations themselves. Fences were built around the reservation schools to separate the students from the reservation Indians, and to keep the children from running away.

Failures of the Reservation System

Although the government was impressed with the apparent success of the boarding schools, it was not pleased with developments on the reservations themselves. The Indians still refused to cooperate with reservation agents. They simply would not convert to Christianity and adopt "American" ways.

In many cases the conditions of reservation life intensified the Indians' resistance to efforts at assimilation. For example, many treaties had stipulated that the government would give the Indians provisions and supplies, such as farming equipment and grain seed, while they were learning how to farm and raise livestock. But these treaties were often not honored. The supplies that did get through to the Indians often turned out to be useless. The farm implements issued were frequently unsuited to the necessary work; Indians who tried to farm would have to plow hard soil with hoes or other inadequate tools. Grain seed was often weedy.

Food provisions were equally inadequate. Often the Indians had to go to the reservation agent's headquarters, usually located near a fort, to get their rations. As they arrived, the Indians would see the fort's ample supplies—grain in bins and cattle in corrals. Then the Indians would be issued their own meager and low-

At some boarding schools, Indian children such as these received not only uniforms that seemed strange to them but new and unfamiliar names as well.

quality provisions by the reservation agent. Such treatment intensified Indian resentment of the reservation system.

Furthermore, the government's payment for Indian lands, though guaranteed in the treaties ceding those lands, was often delayed through financial mismanagement. It took a certain amount of time simply for the Senate to ratify the treaties. But in many cases, payment for Indian land was withheld for five years or more. Indians who had hoped to use these treaty funds to pay for housing and other necessities were sadly disappointed.

On the reservations, missionaries forced the Indians to attend churches, reservation agents and soldiers took Indian children off to school, and settlers illegally moved onto Indian land. Unable to leave the reservation because of government restrictions, and unable to make a living on the reservation, the Indians were in an impossible position.

As early as 1879 Congress considered the possibility of doing away with Indian reservations. The argument was that until the Indians were placed on individual "family-sized" tracts of land they never would become farmers or workers. Supporters of this position maintained that the very idea of a reservation, with land owned communally, was in opposition to American philosophy. It was also argued that on the reservations the Indians could never become "civilized."

This argument, however, was mistaken. The experience of the Cherokees in Oklahoma is a case in point. One Senator who visited them reported that

they have a principal chief and a written constitution, and a legislature elected once in four years; it is composed of a senate and a house. They have a supreme court, a county court, and a school system of which compulsory education is a feature. . . . They have a high school for girls and one for boys, in buildings that would be respectable in Massachusetts. . . .

The head chief told us that there was not a family in that whole nation that had not a home of its own. There was not a pauper in that nation, and the nation did not owe a dollar. . . .

THE POLICY OF LAND ALLOTMENT

The desire to make land available for white settlers was an important factor in the ultimate scrapping of the reservation system. The early railroads had already demonstrated their importance to the economy, and Congress deeded huge tracts of land to railroad corporations in order to encourage new construction. The development of the railroads brought great numbers of people into the West, where most Indian reservations were located. The new settlers of course wanted land for farms and ranches.

By the late 1880's there was a growing realization that Civilization and Christianization had been largely ineffective. Also, there were increasing demands on Congress to make more land available for white settlement. In response, Congress passed the *General Allotment Act,* also known as the Dawes Act, in 1887. The Allotment Act initiated a new Indian policy in the United States. Now each Indian was to be given title to a tract of land, and reservations were gradually to disappear. The Allotment Act was hailed as a legislative landmark by its supporters. However, it was not without its critics. One of the Senators opposing the idea of allotment then observed that the

real aim of this bill is to get at the Indian lands and open them up to settlement. The provisions for the apparent benefit of the Indian are but the pretext to get at his lands and occupy them. . . . If this were done in the name of greed, it would be bad enough; but to do it in the name of humanity, and under the cloak of an ardent desire to promote the Indian's welfare by making him like ourselves, whether he will or not, is infinitely worse.

The General Allotment Act contained four basic provisions. First, the President could ignore all previous laws establishing reservations whenever he felt it would be beneficial to give Indians tracts (allotments) of land or to open the rest of the reservation to settlers. Second, when reservation lands were allotted to individual Indians, the Indians would be given first choice of the allotments; but if they refused to make a choice, federal agents were to choose for them. Third, the allotments to individual Indians would be held in trust by the federal government for twenty-five years. Only then would the Indian receive title to his parcel of land. Fourth, Indians accepting allotments were to be granted American citizenship.

Some Congressmen genuinely believed that the General Allotment Act would help the Indian. Their beliefs were naive. As soon as the act was passed in 1887, land speculators pressured the President to open a number of reservations for settlement. Senator Dawes, who had sponsored the act, responded to these developments with surprise:

President Cleveland said that he did not intend, when he signed the bill, to apply it to more than one reservation at first . . . which I thought was very wise. But you see he has been led to apply it to half a dozen. The . . . greed of the landgrabber is such as to press the application of this bill to the utmost. This will come most rapidly—too rapidly, I think. The greed and hunger and thirst of the white man for the Indian's land is . . . going to press it forward too fast.

The General Allotment Act was implemented in several steps. First, the reservation territory was surveyed into sections of 640 acres. Then the sections were divided into portions. Next, the federal Indian agent conducted a census to determine the reservation's population. The agent announced to the Indians that they could file real estate claims with him. The head of each Indian family could claim a quarter section (160 acres), and each single adult could claim 80 acres. When the Indians' claims had been filed, or—if they were not filed—when the Indians had been assigned land, the agent would then declare all unclaimed reservation land to be surplus. This surplus was to be sold on a first-come, first-served basis. A date for the sale was soon set, and descriptions of the available land were provided to all interested people.

Failings of the Allotment Act

The program was meant to protect the Indians by giving them first choice of the reservation lands. But the Indians were rarely protected in fact. Few of the reservation Indians understood either the English language or the Allotment Act. As a result, even if they were told to file claims, they seldom knew what to do. And apparently some agents did not notify reservation Indians of their rights. In most cases it was the federal agent's responsibility to assign land to the Indians. An agent who was sympathetic to the Indians would make just decisions. But an agent who considered the Indians to be "heathen savages" would not likely give Indians the best land. Furthermore, the agents were often bribed by land-hungry settlers.

Here is an example of the way in which the allotment process was used to promote the interests of land speculators at the expense of the Indians. It comes from a report by a member of the Board of Indian Commissioners. This Board member investigated land allotment procedures at the White Earth Reservation in Minnesota. The Ojibwa Indians on this reservation had been notified that allotment would take place. However, lumber companies were very much interested in the land. Fearful that the Indians might be given some of the best timber land, the lumber companies sent representatives to meet with the federal agent before allotments were made. The agent held "long conferences" with the lumber company representatives in his office. The Commissioner concluded,

What was said behind the closed doors no one knows, but what occurred at the time of the alloting sheds a little light on the situation. . . . My two investigations on the reservation, covering nearly seventeen weeks, led me to believe that the most valuable tracts were selected in advance. . . . It early in the day became evident that the full-bloods were, if possible, to be kept from getting any land. . . .

You will remember that according to the General Allotment Act, Indians receiving land allotments did not receive title to their lands for twenty-five years. They were therefore prevented from selling their land immediately. This provision served two purposes. One was to induce the Indian to remain on his land and begin to farm. The other was to protect him against crafty settlers and land speculators who might try to take the land away from him.

Congress compromised this aspect of the act in 1891. In that year, a revision permitted the Indians to lease their land to the settlers. The new law practically destroyed the Allotment Act's sole redeeming feature. In 1906, Congress authorized a complete revision of the act. Not only could allotted lands now be leased at any time within the twenty-five year period; they could be sold outright as well. It need hardly be said that it was the land speculator, and not the Indian, who always profited from such transactions.

The Allotment Act and its subsequent revisions provided settlers with the land they wanted. But the land was won at the expense of the Indians. By 1902, Indian land holdings had been reduced to nearly half of what they were in 1887. In 1887, some 138 million acres of land were reservation property; by 1902 more than 60 million acres of this land had come under the ownership of settlers and land speculators. Most of the land allotments and sales occurred in the Great Lakes, Plains, and Pacific Coast regions. The Intermountain area and the Southwest were generally unaffected, but only because reservation land there was largely unproductive and therefore unattractive to settlers.

INDIAN REACTION TO ALLOTMENT

The Indian response to the Allotment Act and its revisions was unremittingly negative. As they had done before in similar situations, some of the Indians resorted to violence. Others fled. But most significantly, the Allotment Act caused the appearance of new forms of Indian resistance to government policies.

Passive Resistance in Indian Communities

One method of counteracting the allotment policies was *passive resistance*. Passive resistance is a nonviolent refusal to obey a society's regulations.

What took place on the Sisseton Reservation in South Dakota is an example of passive resistance. The federal agent stationed there in 1879 reported that the Indians had "a friendly feeling toward the government and also the whites" and expressed a willingness "to learn better how to manage their agricultural work." Twenty years later a federal agent reported that about half the tribe no longer wanted to work. And ten years later still, in 1909, about eighty percent of the Indians refused to farm. At Sisseton the Indians chose passive resistance to oppose policies which they knew were unfair.

The events at Sisseton were duplicated by Indians throughout the nation. Many white Americans, unable to understand the reasons behind such Indian refusals to work, accused the Indians of laziness. This accusation might have been justified in some cases, but certainly not in most. Indians recognized the virtue and value of work. It was undoubtedly difficult for many of them to choose not to farm the land, especially for those who had traditionally practiced agriculture. It was unquestionably difficult to become the object of scorn and to endure punishment by federal agents. But apparently many Indians felt that the time for such resistance had come.

The Indians' Rediscovery of Their Heritage

Another form of resistance was religious and philosophical in nature. On many different reservations, religious revivals began to appear. Many Indians stressed the need to renew their traditional ceremonial practices. Missionaries and federal agents often broke up these meetings and arrested the religious leaders.

Two religious movements deserve special attention. One of these, known as the *Ghost Dance,* was eventually destroyed. The other movement, even though it was bitterly opposed by many Americans, continued to grow. In 1944 it was formalized as the *Native American Church.* It is valuable to look briefly at each of these religious movements.

In Nevada during the 1880's, a Paiute Indian known as Wovoka had a vision of a new world which was about to be revealed to man. A great cataclysm was coming, in which the white men would be utterly destroyed. The Indians would regain their traditional lands, their ancestors would return from the dead, and Indian life would again be peaceful and productive. But this new world would not come unless the Indians prepared for it by abstaining from tobacco and alcohol and by leading "honorable" lives. In addition, Indians would have to partake in a night-time ceremony that included songs and a special dance. The teachings of Wovoka spread rapidly among the tribes. According to Edward H. Spicer,

As tribes through the west heard rumors [about Wovoka's ideas], they sent delegations to visit [him]. Wovoka received one delegation after another, explaining his teaching, and demonstrated the dance to them. Kiowas, Cheyennes, Arapahos, and others who had been placed on reservations . . . sent investigators. In many instances they themselves returned to preach.

Many of the Indians in the Plains fervently hoped for the natural catastrophe of which Wovoka had spoken. But the missionaries disapproved of the ceremonies. Missionaries began to publicize what they thought to be the horrors of the Ghost Dance. Their interpretation of the Ghost Dance was inaccurate. The movement was in fact peaceful and highly spiritual, but the sensational publicity it received produced fear that the Ghost Dance would lead to Indian violence.

Finally, in 1890, soldiers who had been influenced by the missionaries' ideas killed some three hundred Sioux Indians who had gathered to participate in a Ghost Dance ceremony. The Indians were unarmed and incapable of fighting back. This inexcusable slaughter occurred at Wounded Knee Creek in South Dakota. After 1890, participation in the Ghost Dance was practically nonexistent. Indians heard what had happened at Wounded Knee Creek, and reservation agents suppressed all efforts at the ceremony's revival.

About the same time, another religious movement started in the southern Plains among Comanche and Wichita Indians. This movement rapidly spread north and west, and within fifty years its ceremonies appeared on all of the reservations in the United States. The movement became known as the *peyote cult* because of the ceremonial use of a cactus product called peyote, which induced hallucinations.

The emphasis in this movement was essentially philosophical. The ceremonies encouraged the individual participants, regardless of their individual backgrounds, to apply the moral aspects of their heritage to the world they lived in. The stress was on the replacement of hatred with forgiveness, of discord with unity, and the renewal of harmony, particularly among Indians, but also between Indians and white Americans. Participation in the ceremonies was never limited to Indians. However, white Americans, whose traditions were different from the Indians', frequently found Indian culture difficult to understand.

Missionaries and other people in the United States consistently attempted to prevent the movement from speading. When efforts to outlaw the use of peyote on reservations proved largely ineffective, opponents of the movement began a publicity campaign which suggested that peyote was extremely dangerous. But in spite of efforts to stop it, the movement spread rapidly. The popularity of the Native American Church, as the peyote cult has been known since 1944, is especially impressive because the movement has not proselytized; that is, it has not actively recruited members.

Another type of resistance movement arising out of the Allotment Act was inspired by American humanitarian groups. Prior to the 1880's these groups had largely ignored Indian people. But by the 1890's humanitarian groups were actively helping the Indians. Humanitarian groups helped to form both the Indian Rights Association and the American Indian Defense Association. These two organizations represented the beginnings of organized Indian political protest. Indians, especially after 1923, began to work closely with them and soon assumed a dominant role in them.

Reasons Behind Indian Unity

The resistance to the Allotment Act was the product of increased Indian unity. One of the intentions of the Allotment Act had been to separate Indians from their groups. But various circumstances minimized the effects of this policy. One of these circumstances was the inter-Indian unity that emerged at the off-reservation boarding schools. Teachers at these schools attempted to prevent their students from talking about Indian culture and traditions. Students who were caught doing this were even punished and isolated. But such discussions still occurred frequently. Friendships developed between students. After their boarding school experience, many students returned to their reservations with new ideas. Indians from different reservations who had been students together visited and wrote letters to each other. Indians soon learned that they shared many problems. Ultimately, unified Indian protest emerged, and some abuses in Indian policy were finally corrected.

With the beginning of American involvement in World War I, Indian students in boarding schools were encouraged to enlist in the United States armed forces. Many did so, and a kind of fraternity was created in which Indians of various backgrounds were brought together. Ideas were exchanged in the army just as they were in the boarding schools. When the troops were discharged at the end of the war, many Indian veterans helped to unify their people.

THE LEGACY OF RESISTANCE

Indian resistance to the Allotment Act began to produce tangible results in the 1920's. In 1924 Congress granted citizenship to all Indians. In addition, between 1920 and 1928 Congress authorized a number of studies of Indian problems. In 1927 Congress commissioned a study by the Institute for Government Research. This organization carefully observed conditions on reservations over a seven-month period, and it presented its findings and recommendations in a document known as the *Meriam Report*. It is impossible to summarize the Meriam Report adequately because it is a very complex document. Below is a sampling of some of its more acute observations.

An overwhelming majority of the Indians are poor, even extremely poor, and they are not adjusted to the economic and social system of the dominant white civilization....
    The health of the Indians as compared with that of the general population is bad....

The prevailing living conditions among the great majority of the Indians are conducive to the development and spread of disease. . . .

The income of the typical Indian family is low and the earned income extremely low. . . . Many of them are living on lands from which a trained and experienced white man could scarcely wrest a reasonable living. . . .

The work of the government directed toward the education and advancement of the Indian himself . . . is largely ineffective . . . .

The survey staff finds itself obliged to say frankly and unequivocally that the provisions for the care of Indian children in boarding schools are grossly inadequate. . . . The question may very properly be raised as to whether much of the work of Indian children in boarding schools would not be prohibited in many states by the child labor laws. . . .

The Indian Service has not appreciated the fundamental importance of family life and community activities in the social and economic development of [Indians]. The tendency has been rather toward weakening Indian family life and community activities than toward strengthening them. . . .

Congress received the Meriam Report in 1928. Its recommendations, however, were generally ignored. In the elections of 1928 many of the Congressmen who had voted to commission the report were replaced with exceptionally conservative legislators. Congress did approve an increase in funds for Indian education, and it reaffirmed the need for day schools on Indian reservations. But this was the extent of Congressional action in 1928. Nothing was done about the Allotment Act.

Similarly, United States citizenship did not immediately bring full rights to all Indians. Voting regulations were still the concern of the individual states. Most states, particularly those in the East, allowed Indians to vote. However, many western states continued to deny Indians this right on the grounds that Indians had long been "wards" of the federal government. As such, it was argued, they were not really full citizens. Some states continued to deny Indians these rights until 1948.

THE INDIAN REORGANIZATION ACT

The Meriam Report, which documented the shortcomings of the Allotment Act, did become the basis for Indian policy reform in the early 1930's. First, Congress abolished the Board of Indian Commissioners, which had approved the Civilization and Christianization policy and the General Allotment Act. Then, in 1933,

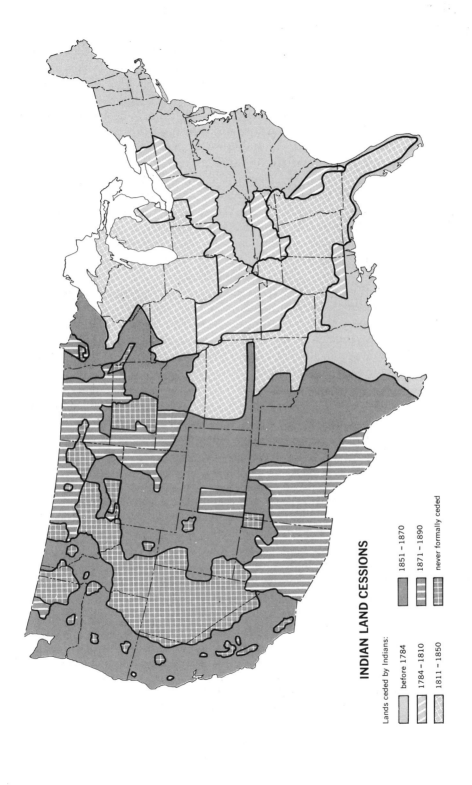

INDIAN LAND CESSIONS

Lands ceded by Indians:

- before 1784
- 1784 – 1810
- 1811 – 1850
- 1851 – 1870
- 1871 – 1890
- never formally ceded

President Franklin D. Roosevelt appointed a former member of the American Indian Defense Association, John Collier, as Commissioner of Indian Affairs. Finally, in 1934, after hearing the recommendations of various committees, Congress approved the *Indian Reorganization Act,* also called the Wheeler-Howard Act.

The new law had four major features. First, it ended land allotment. Second, it established a loan fund to support Indian corporations and to aid students enrolled in industrial schools, high schools, and colleges. Third, it gave Indians on reservations the right to organize themselves into legally recognized groups with written constitutions. These newly organized groups could hire their own lawyers, file suit to defend their lands, and negotiate with federal, state, and local governments. Finally, the Reorganization Act would "not apply to any reservation" where the Indians voted against its application.

Within four years, eighty-five separate Indian groups had adopted constitutions, and more than one hundred others were in the process of preparing them. Federal agents were available to assist Indians in drafting such constitutions. Typically, the form of government that resulted was much like that of the United States. A chairman and a tribal council were to be elected every four years by a majority of the popular vote. Candidates for these offices were selected through a nomination process which included primary elections.

The number of Indian groups that accepted the Reorganization Act indicates that approval of the new federal policy was common. However, the Reorganization Act was rejected in at least seventy-three instances. A brief analysis of one such case, that of the Navajos of the Southwest, is highly suggestive of the reason why support was not unanimous.

The Navajo Reservation was established in 1868. In 1921, after oil was discovered on the reservation, the federal government urged the formation of a Navajo tribal council. In theory this tribal council was to be representative of the Navajo people. However, the Navajos were largely unfamiliar with democratic elections. The tribal council became little more than a device by which the federal government obtained approval for its various programs. For ten years after it first met in 1923, the tribal council was generally unknown on the Navajo Reservation. According to one federal agent, the Navajo people did not realize until 1933 that a tribal council even existed.

The Navajo people were finally introduced to their tribal council in 1933, when the federal government revealed that the Navajo Reservation was severely overgrazed. The government insisted that the number of sheep and goats, estimated to be about one million, had to be reduced by fifty percent. Government agents persuaded the tribal council to approve and carry out the stock reduction program. Navajo sheep owners were told that many of their livestock would have to be destroyed. They were then offered payment for these animals. One observer, Robert W. Young, writes, "The effect [of this program on the Navajos] was one of shock, a reaction stemming from a deep-seated respect by the traditional Navajos of the right to existence shared by all life forms, in combination with an aversion to what appeared as willful waste of the resources upon which they depended for a livelihood."

Thus when the Navajo people were told, the next year, that the United States had developed a program by which they could form their own government, many reacted with suspicion and distrust. The Navajos had learned how federal agents had created a tribal council for them without their knowledge, and they were all too familiar with at least one of its recent decisions. In June 1935, the Navajo people voted against the Indian Reorganization Act.

The Problems of Indian Reorganization

During the late 1930's many of the Indians who had given early approval to the Indian Reorganization Act began to doubt its usefulness. True, the federal loan fund provided Indians with an opportunity to start businesses; more than fifty Indian groups quickly developed their own programs. Some purchased cattle and started dairy and ranching operations; others began large-scale farming activities. The Indians were also aware that they were no longer to be persecuted by missionaries and federal agents for observing their own religious practices. In some cases the government even encouraged the renewal of ceremonial activities.

These were encouraging changes. But in fact the United States' basic Indian policy had not been significantly altered by the Indian Reorganization Act. Indians were still powerless subjects of the United States. The tribal councils, for all practical purposes, had no authority. The federal government continued to take Indian land for use by non-Indians. Furthermore, the federal government used the new Indian governments for its own purposes. Consider the following case in point.

John Collier, who had been appointed Commissioner of Indian Affairs in 1933, strongly maintained that Indian tribal councils should have broad authority. This attitude was evident in many of the decisions he made. In an attempt to restrict federal authority, Collier reduced the number of Bureau of Indian Affairs personnel on the reservations. He transferred some of the responsibilities of the Bureau to other agencies. The Public Health Service, the Forest Service, the Department of Agriculture, and state educational systems all became involved in reservation activities.

But Collier's plan produced results wholly unrelated to his intentions. When agents from the various federal and state offices appeared, Indians discovered that the influence of the tribal councils over reservation government actually decreased. The demands and regulations imposed by the new officials effectively negated many of the tribal councils' proposals.

Further Shortcomings of Reorganization

In the Reorganization Act the federal government had approved the cessation of land allotments. It gave the tribal councils the power to prevent the sale or lease of tribal lands. After 1934, however, these provisions of the Reorganization Act were weakened in several ways.

In an act approved by Congress in 1938 the government assumed the right to lease Indian land for mining purposes, "by authority of the tribal council or other authorized spokesmen." The phrase "other authorized spokesmen" implied that federal administrators on the reservations could recommend that leases be issued. The federal power of *eminent domain,* that is, the right of the government to take over land for the benefit of the general public, was applied to Indian reservations in spite of the Reorganization Act of 1934.

The government's decision to resettle some of the Indians from northern Arizona on a tract of land along the Colorado River in southwestern Arizona is illustrative. In this case the land in question was already part of the Colorado River Indian Reservation. It belonged to another group of Indians. The Indians from northern Arizona were forced to become members of the Colorado River Tribes regardless of the opinions of the Colorado River Indian Tribal Council.

The Indian Reorganization Act was ineffective in yet another way. Soil conservation and land reclamation programs were carried out on Indian lands by several different agencies of the federal government. These agencies were not associated with the Bureau of Indian Affairs. In many cases they began to work on reservation lands without securing permission from the tribal councils. In other cases the tribal councils were simply notified that the work was going to be done.

The soil conservation and land reclamation programs provided employment for many people. But few of the employees were Indians. In fact, the employment programs were frequently developed at the expense of Indians. This was true even in employment programs directly connected with the Bureau of Indian Affairs.

Section twelve of the Indian Reorganization Act had specified that "qualified Indians [shall be given] preference [in] appointment to vacancies." However, there was in fact no real attempt made to recruit Indians. Commissioner Collier argued that the number of non-Indian employees in the Bureau of Indian Affairs should be reduced. His argument was not accepted, however, and the number of non-Indian employees actually increased in the 1930's.

Perhaps the Indian Reorganization Act eventually would have produced a better way of life for the Indian people. Many of the Indian groups were suspicious of it, and it was severely criticized by some Congressmen—one called it a "dangerous, Christ-mocking, communistic-aiding, subversive set-up." But Indians did use the act to achieve some of their goals. The advent of World War II, however, more or less stopped the implementation of the act, and by the time the war came to an end, the Indian Reorganization Act had been forgotten.

INDIAN POLICY AFTER WORLD WAR II

In World War II, about twenty-five thousand Indians served in the United States armed forces. In addition, approximately forty thousand Indians left the reservations to work in factories or take other jobs connected with the war effort. These figures indicate the high degree to which the Indian people were willing to cooperate with the United States. Other Indians, who for various reasons could not leave their reservations, supported and participated in voluntary local war efforts, as did Americans throughout the nation.

Despite the sacrifices that Indians made, the federal government did little to correct the abuses in its Indian policy after the war. In fact, in the postwar period Congress adopted a policy that was more in line with the Allotment Act than with the Reorganization Act. The first step in this new policy came in 1946, with the establishment of an *Indian Claims Commission*. This Commission was to rule on claims for lands which Indians felt had been taken from them illegally. If the Commission ruled in favor of the Indians, the federal government was obligated to pay a fair price for the land. Some fair rulings were made, but the Indian Claims Commission also provided the federal government with the means with which to deprive Indian reservation councils of their responsibilities.

The emergence of the Indian Claims Commission was originally interpreted as a major step toward self-government. But by 1950 it became obvious that the Indian Claims Commission was detrimental to the welfare of Indians. The Commission's decisions were preparing the way, not for Indian self-government, but simply for the termination and abolition of reservations and tribal governments. The Indians' worst fears were confirmed in 1953 when Congress passed *Resolution 108*. The resolution stipulated, "It is the policy of Congress, as rapidly as possible, to make the Indians . . . subject to the same laws and entitled to the same privileges and responsibilities as are applicable to other citizens of the United States. . . ."

The Termination Policy

Resolution 108 directed the Department of the Interior, which included the Bureau of Indian Affairs, to recommend a program by which certain Indian groups could be immediately "freed from federal supervision and control." Some groups were named specifically, such as the Flathead tribe of Montana and the Menominees of Wisconsin. But many other Indians were mentioned in a more general way. For example, "all the Indian tribes and the individual members thereof" in California, Florida, New York, and Texas were included in the resolution's instructions. During the 1953–54 session of Congress, three bills were introduced pertaining to the abolition of federal services for Ute and Paiute Indians.

Indians from twenty-one states went to Washington to protest the adoption of these *termination* bills. As the hearings progressed, nation-wide support for the Indian position grew. One journalist, writing in *The Christian Century*, stated that termination bills

do more than withdraw federal trust from Indian properties. . . . They also terminate the application of the Indian Reorganization Act of 1934, abolish tribal constitutions and corporations based on that law, abrogate federal-Indian treaties, and impose the breakup of tribal properties into individual parcels. But the basis of the Indian's apprehension is that these bills threaten his land. He remembers what happened as a result of the Indian Allotment Act of 1887. . . .

Congress rejected the arguments of the Indian groups and their supporters. Glenn Emmons, who was the Commissioner of Indian Affairs during the period of termination legislation, defended the legislation in a 1958 report. He said that termination was "one of the most valuable and salutary Congressional measures we have had in Indian Affairs for a great many years."

Many of the persons who defended termination claimed that it was merely a restatement of the principles of the Reorganization Act. Termination and reorganization, they claimed, had both been designed to lead the Indian groups toward self-government. The advocates of termination maintained that Indian self-government was slow in coming under the Reorganization Act because of federal interference and red tape. Resolution 108, it was said, gave the Indian at once what the Reorganization Act would have taken years to produce.

The termination program developed by the Bureau of Indian Affairs operated as follows. First, the various reservation administrators would decide which groups were ready for termination. When a group was selected, the tribal council of that group would be notified and directed to prepare a "tribal roll." Reservation land was then divided equally. Each resident of the reservation would be given title to his property. Each Indian was free to do as he wished with his property. The entire process was to take no more than five years for each reservation. By 1961 some forty-seven reservations either had been or were in the process of being terminated. This affected Indian groups in California, Oregon, Nevada, Utah, Texas, South Dakota, Wisconsin, and South Carolina.

Termination was accompanied by an emphasis on education. New boarding schools were built on several reservations. A major effort at enrolling Indian children in state public schools was launched. Adults were encouraged to participate in classes in reading, writing, and industrial skills. A relocation program was introduced. By its terms, Indians could be transferred from reservations to certain cities, such as Chicago, Denver, Albuquerque, and Los Angeles, where they could receive on-the-job training in industry.

In 1953 Congress also passed what is known as *Public Law 280*. This law permitted five states—California, Minnesota, Nebraska, Oregon, and Wisconsin—to extend their jurisdiction over Indian reservations within their territories. An amendment to the law permitted other states to be included if they wished. Where state legislatures agreed to implement the law, Indians on reservations in those states were deprived of almost all tribal council authority.

Termination in the 1960's

In the early 1960's the American public showed a new sensitivity to the manner in which Indians had been treated. There was growing pressure on Congress for a reappraisal of Indian policy. The cases of the Menominee and Klamath groups, who were left poverty-stricken and landless by termination, were well publicized. They roused the American people from their ignorance and apathy. Though no new legislation was drafted by Congress, termination did occur less frequently. Additional time was granted to the reservations already in the process of termination. The Bureau of Indian Affairs discouraged reservation administrators from starting new termination efforts.

In 1960 President Eisenhower authorized a task force for the study of Indian policy and programs, to be appointed by the Department of the Interior. The task force was directed to analyze Indian policy and make recommendations for its improvement.

The report of this task force was made public in 1961. It stated that Congress should help the Bureau of Indian Affairs achieve three objectives: "1. Maximum Indian economic self-sufficiency. 2. Full participation of Indians in American life. 3. Equal citizenship privileges and responsibilities for Indians." In conclusion the task force emphasized

that the aid of the tribe—or, more properly, the Indian community—is crucial to the achievement of these objectives and this support should be secured ·before projects are commenced. The Indians can retain their tribal identities and much of their culture while working toward a greater adjustment and, for the further enrichment of our society, it is in our best interests to encourage them to do so.

Congress graciously accepted the report of the task force but suggested no changes in policy. But when the *Economic Opportunity Act* was approved in August 1964, initiating the "War on Poverty," a special Indian program was developed by the Office of Economic Opportunity. Indian groups were encouraged to use funds provided by the Economic Opportunity Act. Many responded. By 1965, programs were begun in community development, job training, legal aid, and other areas. These programs were designed by the Indians themselves. Several Indian groups also developed their own educational methods with funds furnished by the Economic Opportunity Act. Some courses emphasized the teaching of tribal traditions to both adults and children. Others stressed the Indian's heritage in North America. At least two significant educational innovations were developed by the Navajo people with Economic Opportunity Act funds. One of these was a Navajo-operated elementary school. The other was a two-year college administered and staffed by Navajo people and located on reservation land.

The policy of termination, however, persisted in the 1960's. Occasionally Congress demanded termination actions in return for federal payments to Indians.

This happened to the Senecas, for instance, in connection with the building of the Kinzua Dam in western New York State. The planned reservoir would flood a great portion of the Senecas' reservation. When their efforts to prevent the dam's construction failed, the Senecas asked for funds to pay for the flooded lands. But Congress refused to honor the tribe's claim until the Senecas promised never to make any further demands on the federal government. Of course, this was precisely what the termination act was designed to accomplish.

The development of oil resources in Alaska in the late 1960's encouraged Congress to try to find the ultimate solution to the Indian land "problem." In 1970, in a statement on Indian policy, President Nixon stressed that the Indians in the United States should determine their own affairs. In his statement the President denounced termination. Nixon's speech was a source of encouragement, since it gave hope that the American government would become more sensitive to the needs of the nation's Indian population.

In 1870 the United States was anxious to help the Indian become a part of American society, supposedly so that he could enjoy the benefits of civilization. One hundred years later the United States was still trying to "help the Indian." There are many reasons why these efforts failed. One reason in particular deserves attention.

Consider the impression that the Indian received of the society he was supposed to prefer to his own. To the Indian this society must have appeared filled with inconsistencies. First it confined him to a reservation; a few years later it encouraged him to leave the reservation. For a time it prohibited him from practicing his own religious ceremonies; suddenly it encouraged him to teach these ceremonies to others. At various times it opposed, then supported, and then tried again to abolish Indian self-government. For years it outlawed the use of Indian languages; then it stressed the value of Indian languages. It kidnapped children and put them in schools; then, once the children were away, it told the Indian it encouraged family life.

Traditionally, Indian societies were consistent. Indians had adapted successfully to their environment, and their life styles persisted through centuries. Indians had defined their values clearly. It is not difficult to understand their reluctance to part with their heritage.

The failure of the United States government's Indian policy has had tragic effects on the Indian people. After a century of "showing and telling" the Indians about Western civilization, a few facts were painfully evident. For example, according to a 1971 report on Indian reservations by the Department of Commerce, the median annual income for reservation families was about $3,000. On some reservations the median family income was as little as $1,400 for the year.

Unemployment on Indian reservations averaged 45 percent in 1970. (By comparison, the national unemployment level was about 5 percent during the same period.) The average amount of schooling for Indians on reservations in 1970 was less than seven years. Schooling levels on a few reservations were reported to be less than four years.

In 1970 the average life expectancy for United States citizens as a whole was about 70 years. But Indian life expectancy was less than two thirds as high—only 44 years. More than three out of every four reservation Indians lived in inadequate housing, according to federal government standards. Only a small percentage (about 20 percent) of the houses on Indian reservations had indoor plumbing or nearby water sources.

SUGGESTED FURTHER READING

Brown, Dee, *Bury My Heart at Wounded Knee: An Indian History of the American West*. New York: Holt, Rinehart & Winston, 1970.

Fritz, Henry E., *The Movement for Indian Assimilation, 1860–1960*. Philadelphia: University of Pennsylvania Press, 1963.

Jackson, Donald, *Custer's Gold*. New Haven: Yale University Press, 1966.

Josephy, Alvin M., Jr., *The Indian Heritage of America*. New York: Alfred A. Knopf, 1968.

McNickle, D'Arcy, *They Came Here First*. Philadelphia: J. B. Lippincott, 1949.

Spicer, Edward H., *A Short History of the Indians of the United States*. New York: Van Nostrand Reinhold, 1969.

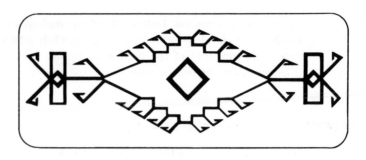

a case study:

CONTEMPORARY NAVAJO RESERVATION LIFE

The federal government's Bureau of Indian Affairs supervises about 250 Indian reservations throughout the United States. These range in size from a tiny, one-acre parcel of land in California to the huge, 14-million-acre Navajo Reservation in Arizona, New Mexico, and Utah. These reservations, together with a number of state reservations, are the home of over 350,000 Indians in the United States.

There is a great deal of misinformation and misunderstandanding about conditions on Indian reservations. Some critics have described reservations as being similar to concentration camps. Others have given the impression that Indians receive monthly checks from the government, pay no taxes, and have no obligations. Neither of these conceptions is true. The Navajo Reservation provides an example of the kind of conditions that actually exist.

Navajo Attitudes About the Reservation

One of the Navajo legends explains that this is the "fifth world" in which Navajos have lived. The legend tells how the Navajos have passed through one dangerous world after another searching for a place of peace and harmony. Finally their revered ancestral leaders led them to their present territory and assured them that there the people would find what they had sought.

The present reservation is a holy land for the many Navajos who believe in this legend. Covering more than 20,000 square miles, the reservation is about the same size as the state of West Virginia. Nearly 100,000 Navajos lived on it permanently in 1970.

Problems of Reservation Life

Although it may be a "holy place," the reservation confronts its residents with serious problems. Poverty is severe and widespread. It is difficult either to raise food or to find a job. Much of the territory is dust-dry land, on which productive farming is impossible. Some sheep and cattle are raised, but these animals rarely grow fat on the sparse grassland. There are only a few small factories and businesses on the reservation, and jobs are scarce. Federal and tribal programs provide some employment but, according to the Department of Commerce, more than 50 percent of the Navajo work force was unemployed in 1971. The average reservation family earned less than $2,500 in that year.

Disease is another serious problem. Homes rarely have plumbing, and the water is often unsafe to drink. Tuberculosis, pneumonia, influenza, and trachoma are common illnesses. Infant mortality rates on the reservations are much higher than they are in the rest of the nation. Life expectancy for the Navajo is less than 50 years.

The Navajos also face threats to their traditions, as more and more of their children attend schools and learn the language and ways of non-Indian society. Reservation land itself is constantly menaced by state governments and private interests. Problems are inescapable on the reservation.

Rewards of Reservation Life

If life on the reservation is so insecure, why do the Navajo people live there? Why don't they move somewhere else? Non-Indians have been perplexed by these questions. Another look at the Navajo Reservation offers a clue to the answers.

In the first place, the reservation is the Navajos' homeland. For generations they have defended its boundaries against foreign encroachments. Their people held on to it through periods of Spanish,

Mexican, and American domination of the Southwest. Although many Navajos were captured and forced to leave the territory by United States troops in 1864, they returned to the area four years later, in 1868. The Navajos have never wanted to leave their land; this feeling has not changed.

The belief that the reservation is a holy place is another reason Navajos choose to live there. It was the land selected by their revered ancestral leaders. Prominent mountains guard its sanctity. Many of the springs and streams, hills and valleys, rock and sand formations have religious meaning. The land supplies Navajo medicine men with plant pollens, fibers, particular kinds of sand, and other materials that they use for curing their people's spiritual and physical diseases.

Furthermore, loneliness is unknown by the Navajos who live on the reservation. Friends are to be found everywhere, and because of the Navajo social system, so are relatives. Someone always has food for a person who is hungry or help for a person in trouble. A Navajo cannot remain discouraged for long, because friends are always nearby with sympathy and encouragement.

Often overlooked, but nevertheless very important, is the unparalleled scenic beauty of the region. In some places, dense pine forests hover protectively around tiny azure lakes. In other places, huge sandstone monoliths jut hundreds of feet into the sky from table-flat plains. Striking scenic contrasts are everywhere: high mountains and deep canyons, green meadows and sandy flatlands, dark forests and sunlit deserts. Few places in the world are more awesome than the Navajo Reservation.

The Navajo Family

The family is the basic social unit of any human group. In the family, children learn the language and values of their society.

The Navajo family usually contains a large number of people. This is because of the way Navajo society defines the family. To the Navajos the family includes all the people who are related through the female relatives. Thus a Navajo child's family might include not only his parents and his brothers and sisters, but also his mother's sisters and their children, his mother's mother, and perhaps his own sister's children as well. In most cases these people live near each other. The Navajo child interacts with each of these people as intensively as a non-Indian child does with the members of his much smaller family group.

This family arrangement serves several important purposes for the Navajo. It links him to a large group of people—his clan relatives—who he knows will protect and help him under almost any circumstances. From his family the Navajo child learns that throughout his life, no matter where he is on the reservation, he will never be far from relatives. If he cannot find a job, or if his crops fail, he can always go to his relatives for assistance.

In return, the Navajo child learns from his family that he is needed and important. He is responsible for many other people. A Navajo often shares his income with many relatives; his crops are distributed among many different homes. Any relative who can do so is expected to contribute to the needs of anyone else in his clan group who is in trouble.

The Navajo Community

Most non-Indians in the United States think of a community as a place. The Navajos have a different idea. A community, to them, consists of a group of people who have common ideas and who will cooperate to achieve mutual goals.

Navajos have never placed much value on living close to others. The simple fact that people live close together does not guarantee that they will help one another; people in large towns may not even know their neighbors. Towns, therefore, have never been popular with Navajos. A community on the Navajo Reservation typically spreads out over several square miles.

Navajo communities may appear rather informal and unstructured, but in fact they all share certain characteristics. Each community includes members of several different clan groups. Each community has a leader, or headman, who is carefully selected for his wisdom and his extensive knowledge of Navajo traditions. The headman acts for the benefit of the entire community, settling disputes between community members and representing the community in tribal affairs.

Frequently each community either has its own medicine man or shares one with another community. The medicine man acts to protect the people from various kinds of dangers, to counsel them, and to conduct religious ceremonies for them. Community meetings are often held in conjunction with religious ceremonies.

Community membership is stable and well defined. The members of a group know who belongs and who are outsiders. When a woman marries, for example, and her husband comes to live with her, he is often considered an outsider for several years. Only by his actions and attitude does he eventually succeed in winning acceptance by others in the community.

Navajo Government

Like many other Indian groups, the Navajos had a representative form of government long before outsiders came to teach them about democracy. The community leaders, or headmen, have always represented their groups in important tribal matters. However, this system has been a continual source of conflict in tribal relations with the United States government.

In the 1920's the federal government divided the Navajo Reservation into districts, decreeing that each district was to elect a representative to the newly formed tribal council. But the federal agents who established the districts were unaware of the existing Navajo communities. Consequently the district boundaries did not coincide with the communities, and individual communities were often divided among several districts. Communities often could not be represented by their headmen. As a result, the Navajo people showed little interest in voting, and the tribal councilmen were ultimately chosen by federal agents.

Although the process of electing councilmen has been revised several times since the 1920's, the local communities are still not effectively represented. To many Navajos the tribal council is a "foreign" organization, reflecting the ideas of the federal government instead of Navajo opinions.

Similarities with Rural American Life

To the surprise of many visitors, there are no fences along the border of the Navajo Reservation. Only small signs beside the major highways inform the traveler that he has entered the reservation.

In many respects reservation life is quite similar to life anywhere in the rural United States. During the summer most Navajos are busy farming. Their fields produce grain, vegetables, and alfalfa. Sheep and cattle graze on pasture lands. Reservation rodeos and fairs are popular and well attended.

From fall to summer most Navajo children attend school. The adults who have jobs go off to work each day. Those who are unemployed work around the house or in the community area. On weekends families travel to town to buy groceries or other needed items. They often spend much of the shopping day visiting with friends who have also come to shop. Throughout the year most Navajos keep abreast of national and international affairs through radio, television, newspapers, and news magazines.

Contrasts with Rural American Life

Although the reservation visitor may be impressed with the similarities between the reservation and the rural United States, a closer look reveals major differences. Pickup trucks driven by Navajos frequently carry containers for water. Many Navajo families have neither plumbing nor wells near their homes and have to take water from distant sources. Many Navajos cannot afford trucks or cars. Horse-drawn wagons, most of them equipped with automobile wheels and tires, are not an uncommon sight on the reservation, even in the 1970's. Hundreds of Navajos cannot even afford to keep a horse.

While both reservation children and rural American children attend school, their experiences are quite different. Schools in the rural United States are normally staffed by local people; reservation schools rarely employ Navajos, either as teachers or as administrators. Children in the rural United States read books written in their own language; children on the reservation must learn to read books written in a foreign language, English. The great majority of rural American children return home from school each day. But nearly 19,000 Navajo children attended boarding schools in 1970 and did not come home for weeks at a time.

Underlying the differences in daily activities are serious differences in governmental affairs. The Navajo tribal council has only limited authority over reservation matters. The federal government has frequently promised that Indians will be given more control over their own affairs, but this means little to the reservation population. Tribal budgets are still audited by federal officials—even when the funds to be spent come from the tribe rather than the federal government. Federal laws severely restrict the tribe's water and land-use rights and its income from industrial leases. Furthermore, the state legislatures of New Mexico and Arizona have periodically brought pressures on the tribal government. At one time or another the states have sought additional tax revenues, requested educational authority, or tried to impose voting restrictions on the reservation population.

Navajo Developments in Education

Indians are not required to live on reservations. But many prefer reservation life. Those who have chosen to live on the reservation have tried to retain their heritage in a modern world. A step in this direction has been taken with the development of Navajo-controlled schools. Three of these have recently been organized: Rough Rock Elementary School,

Ramah Navajo High School, and Navajo Community College.

The Rough Rock and Ramah schools are governed by a Navajo school board. The two schools teach the Navajo and English languages, Navajo and United States history, and Navajo as well as non-Indian customs. Both schools encourage applications from Indian teachers and administrators.

Navajo Community College has a two-year degree program. Its course offerings emphasize Indian studies and Navajo studies, in addition to the usual college curriculum. The college sponsors a variety of services for reservation people. It provides agricultural training and consultation, vocational courses, community development assistance, summer programs, and a popular series of lectures by Indians from throughout the United States. Although the college is controlled by and is designed to serve Navajos, its staff and student body is multi-racial.

Navajo communities and the Navajo tribe plan to develop additional school facilities in the future. In the meantime these three schools help to improve the quality of education throughout the reservation by stimulating changes in existing public schools. Visitors from other Indian tribes have come to study the operation of the three schools in preparation for developing their own reservation schools.

The Future of the Reservation Navajo

Most Navajo people believe that reservation life will improve in the future. They are aware of their many problems: continuing population growth, a lack of jobs, and already overused land. But the Navajos are confident that something will happen to correct these problems.

Their faith is not unreasonable. The Navajos have faced and overcome problems in the past. There are many possible solutions for present problems. If they could obtain water, the Navajos could produce high crop yields on their farms. If they could persuade small industries to move to the reservation, there would be wider employment.

Furthermore, the reservation has already produced gas, oil, coal, and uranium. Many Navajos are aware that it contains untapped resources. They hope the day might come when the Navajos, rather than the federal government, will have the power to issue leases and develop the reservation's resources.

But while many Navajos are hopeful about the future, others see danger signs. The chief fear is that the federal government will terminate their reservation or in other ways destroy their hopes for improvement. This fear was underscored in the late 1960's, when the tribal council negotiated leases with coal and power companies, under government pressure.

The coal company has been permitted to strip mine. That is, it has been allowed to strip the soil off large areas of land to get at the coal deposits underneath. This method has rendered thousands of acres of reservation land unfit for future use. Furthermore, the coal is burned at power plants on the reservation to generate electricity for cities in California and Arizona. These coal-burning power plants have darkened the reservation's skies and produced pollution such as the Navajos have never before encountered. Developments like these could put an end to hopes for a better future.

No two reservations in the United States are exactly alike. But many of the problems and rewards are similar on the different reservations. In the company of his own people and living on his own land, an Indian often finds the psychological, social, and spiritual strength necessary for him to retain his individual dignity. At the same time, the reservations are areas of severe poverty, widespread disease, low educational levels, and early death. Aware that the federal government is capable of carrying out extensive health and economic programs elsewhere in the world, Indians can only conclude that they are of little importance in the eyes of the United States government.

The thunderbird, a traditional
symbol, persists in modern
Indian jewelry.

5

INDIAN CULTURE:
ITS PERSISTENCE AND DESTINY

For two hundred years the Indian policy of the United States was based on the assumption that the Indians would either become "civilized" or vanish as a people. Yet it is apparent that the Indians have neither vanished nor become immersed in the "melting pot" of American society. Indian population has more than tripled since 1910. And in the 1970's the traditions and customs of the various Indian groups were widely known and faithfully practiced.

This is not to say that Indians did not change through the years. Indians combined some new social customs with some old ones. They borrowed certain "modern" ideas and united these with their own. From these elements, they fashioned a new kind of existence for themselves. Characteristically "Indian" cultures persisted in spite of the pressure of white settlers, the coercion of American government, and the Indian's own willingness to adopt at least some of the habits of American society. Precisely how these cultures endured is the subject of this chapter.

GROUP PRIDE AMONG THE AMERICAN INDIANS

Group pride is an expression of social identity. Societies with group pride stress the validity of their own traditions, the merit of their own customs, the truth of their own beliefs, and the importance of remaining distinct from other societies.

Each of the many different Indian societies had defined its own culture long ago. As a result, there was a great deal of diversity among the Indian groups in North America. There were many different languages, types of social organization, methods of procuring and producing food, religious ceremonies and beliefs, and philosophies, technologies, and art forms.

This diversity persisted for thousands of years. Nevertheless, each Indian group regarded the cultures and societies of its neighbors with respect. Rival groups did not try to convince each other to adopt different practices. When changes did occur, it was usually because a group realized that changes were necessary, not because of pressure by outsiders.

The Survival of Indian Societies

When the Europeans came to North America, they failed to see the diverse character of Indian societies. To the European settlers, the Indians of North America were all savages. There was little change in this attitude as the United States emerged as a nation. The characteristic opinion of the American public and the United States government was: "If you've seen one Redskin, you've seen 'em all." Because of such attitudes, the tragedies of Indian removal, land allotment, Indian reorganization, and termination were met with apathy by most white Americans. Even as late as 1968 the author of a book that was widely read in the United States observed that "to all intents and purposes the Indian civilization [in the United States] disappeared early in the twentieth century. The conquest has been complete: The Indian was remade in the White's image or else safely bottled up on reservations."

Such blanket generalizations are as inaccurate today as they were in the past. Almost all Indian societies had, and still have, distinctive characteristics. Three factors that contributed to this distinctiveness in most Indian societies were religion, family life, and leadership.

The word "religion" is derived from a Latin word which means "to knit or tie together." Religion, therefore, can be thought of as a social device which knits the various parts of society into a unified whole. Religious teachings explain the past and the future, the known and the unknown, and the visible and the invisible. They reveal the origin of man; they supply moral guidelines; they explain natural catastrophes, disease, and death; and they furnish man with a system that reveals the design of the world and the universe. All religions thus provide man with explanations, and these are very important to any society.

When the future is unclear to members of a society, they often turn to religion for comfort. According to the Old Testament, the Hebrews demonstrated great religious zeal when they were conquered by the Egyptians. Similarly, during World War II, church attendance in America increased.

When Indian societies were harassed by the American government, they too revived their own religious ideas. Traditional ceremonies were held regularly. Children were taught their religious heritage. Men and women were reminded of the moral ideals of their group and were encouraged to practice them. Some Indians believed that they were being mistreated because they had violated taboos, or religious rules. As each society turned more and more to its own religious beliefs, it became increasingly distinctive from others, and this distinctiveness encouraged the further development of group pride.

The activities of the family unit also contributed to group pride. Families provide children with an introduction and orientation to their society. Parents are expected to teach children the language and rules of their society so the children can become productive adult members of the group.

Originally, most Indian societies allowed parents a great deal of time to supervise their children. Children generally remained at home with their parents until they were old enough to start families of their own. Boys and girls spent a great deal of time working with their parents, sharing different responsibilities, and learning how to meet and solve problems.

This tradition was severely disrupted when the Indians were placed on reservations. Now children were being taken from their homes and placed in school. School, particularly the boarding school, deprived the family of its traditional role in molding children's attitudes.

When Indian parents first learned that their children were to be placed in school, they tried to hide them. But concealment was rarely successful, and Indian parents soon approached the problem differently. Instead of introducing the children gradually to the language, social rules, and expectations of the society, families started to provide the children with as much information as possible before they began school. Children were carefully and thoroughly instructed in the language, traditions, and customs of their society as soon as they could possibly understand what they were being taught.

Indian parents were remarkably successful in this effort. Schoolteachers often complained that even the youngest Indian children came to school with a firm understanding of their heritage. The teachers frequently reacted by forbidding the children to use their own languages at school or to talk about their own societies.

As Indian parents began to instruct their children with thoroughness and urgency, Indian groups achieved a new sense of social identity. Interest in community development activities, group meetings, and cultural pride became common.

The third means by which Indian group pride prospered, and by which Indian cultures were preserved, was the recognition of leadership. Most Indian societies (though not all) had leaders. But these leaders usually were not the men whom white Americans regarded as the Indian leaders—the great warriors, such as Crazy Horse, Red Cloud, and Geronimo. Such men were, of course, important and popular, but the day-to-day leaders of Indian groups were traditionally selected on the basis of competence, rather than popularity. Because competence was often equated with experience and wisdom, the old were generally chosen to lead.

This fact, though often overlooked by non-Indians who study Indian society, is extremely important. The selection of old leaders encouraged conservatism in Indian society. Old leaders tended to advise the group to retain old and trusted ways of action instead of accepting new ways. Those who disagreed with the leaders were encouraged to leave the group. This was another way in which distinctiveness of each Indian society endured.

PAN–INDIANISM AND INDIAN UNITY

Group pride, characterized by distinctiveness and diversity among different societies, has been a feature of American Indian societies for a very long time. *Pan-Indianism*, on the other hand, has developed only recently. It emerged when different Indian societies realized that they had common interests and grievances. The movement represents the voluntary cooperation of diverse Indian groups. By the 1970's, Pan-Indianism had three major goals: to improve the treatment the Indians were receiving under federal Indian policy, to create a new atmosphere for Indians in the United States, and to enlighten the American public about Indian affairs.

Efforts at large-scale cooperation by Indian groups began in 1944. In November of that year representatives from more than fifty reservations met in Denver, Colorado, to discuss ways of correcting abuses in federal Indian policy. The representatives decided to form a national organization of Indian tribes. They thought such an organization would be able to bargain more effectively with the United States government.

The new organization was called the *National Congress of American Indians* (NCAI). Its first director, a Cherokee, maintained that the

Federal Government has failed again and again in its dealings with Indians because there has not been any leadership among the Indians, or such leadership was negative and effective only in resisting the Federal policy. Indian leadership should contribute to the formulation of Federal policy. It should take the leading part in inquiring into the needs of Indians and in making those needs vocal.

Within a few years the NCAI began publishing a newsletter. It also supported research into Indian policy abuses. It put pressure on Congressmen to vote for legislation favorable to Indians. It sponsored national and regional Indian conferences. Faced with organized Indian resistance for the first time since the "Indian wars," the federal government threatened members of the organization with retaliation. When tribal groups continued to associate themselves with the NCAI, federal administrators on the reservations terminated federal programs. If the tribes withdrew from the NCAI, they were rewarded with new programs.

The NCAI was legally incorporated in 1954. The same year, according to one of its directors,

A systematic attack on every tribe in the nation [began]. . . . The basic approach of [the federal government] never varied for fourteen years. Unbearable pressures, lies, promises, and threats of termination were made whenever a tribe won funds from the United States because of past swindles by the federal government. Whenever a tribe needed special legislation to develop its resources, termination was often the price asked for the attention.

Such pressure had an adverse effect on the NCAI during the 1960's, and for a time it lost membership and prestige. However, by the early 1970's it appeared ready to assume serious responsibilities in the Pan-Indian movement once more.

In 1961 an all-Indian conference was held at the University of Chicago. Some ninety tribal groups attended. The meeting was called to protest the government's termination policy. It also opposed the implementation of Public Law 280, the 1953 law that gave individual states the right to extend their jurisdiction over Indian reservations.

The conference issued a statement known as the "Declaration of Indian Purpose." Also, it was significant for two additional reasons. First, it was an important stage in the development of the Pan-Indian movement. Second, the conference was instrumental in the formation of another nation-wide Indian organization, the *National Indian Youth Council* (NIYC).

The NCAI had supported a formal and cautious approach to the reform of federal Indian policy. The NIYC was much more aggressive. In contrast to the NCAI's policy, membership in the NIYC was on an individual, rather than a tribal, basis, and branches were established throughout the country.

An event which served to catapult the Youth Council into nation-wide attention occurred in February 1964. It grew out of a meeting of the tribal council of the Makah Indians in the state of Washington. The state legislature, as permitted by Public Law 280, had acted to compel reservation Indians to obey state fishing laws. This action deprived the Indians of an important source of livelihood. Many of them depended on year-round fishing for food.

These Indian youths are demonstrating near
the United Nations Building in New York to
protest the treatment of American Indians.

The Makah Tribal Council decided to protest this legislation, but they recognized the need for wide support if they were to win. They therefore sent word to fifty other reservations and to the NIYC that there would be a mass meeting to test the legality of Public Law 280. The tribal elders asked the young university Indians to lead the activities.

The Fish-Ins were the result. In these demonstrations, groups of Indians fished for salmon in waters that had been guaranteed to them by previous federal treaties, but which had been taken away again by state law and Public Law 280. Arrests and jail sentences followed the Fish-Ins, but the events received nation-wide publicity.

Expanding Protest Activities

In subsequent years this kind of protest activity increased. The NIYC, along with regional Pan-Indian groups, sponsored and participated in demonstrations throughout the country. Groups of Indians moved onto government lands on both coasts. They also occupied Alcatraz Island, in San Francisco Bay, to demonstrate their displeasure with federal Indian policy.

The restoration of fishing rights was hardly the only goal of Pan-Indian groups. Diverse Indian groups also united to obtain a fair share of the wealth of American society. Job discrimination had led to extremely high unemployment rates for Indians both on and off the reservations. In various states Indians were deprived of services available to other people, simply because they were Indians. Until 1965, Indians in some states were still denied voting rights on the basis of literacy requirements.

Concern over their plight led Indians in many areas of the country to organize regional and urban Pan-Indian groups. Indian centers came into existence in large as well as small cities; intertribal clubs were formed in many universities and even in some high schools with high Indian enrollment. The NCAI and the NIYC encouraged and assisted such groups to publicize discrimination against Indians.

The Pan-Indian movement also attempted to educate the American public about Indians. A group called the *American Indian Historical Society* was formed in the 1960's. This group published a monthly magazine, *The Indian Historian,* and encouraged the publication by others of truthful material about Indians. The NCAI helped to distribute publications about Indians to the

American public. National Indian groups and local associations urged high schools and colleges to introduce Indian studies into their curricula. In 1970 one Indian spokesman said, "The public at large [must] drop the myths in which it has clothed us for so long."

THE PRACTICE OF SELECTIVE BORROWING

For two hundred years the United States government operated on the assumption that, given time and the proper kind of encouragement, Indians would gradually assume the "American" way of life. It seemed inconceivable that the Indian could continue to live as he once did after having seen the advantages of "civilization."

When white Americans finally realized that most Indians preferred their own cultures to that of the United States, they concluded that the Indians were strange people indeed. What they did not realize, however, was that the Indians had in fact examined American society and had selectively borrowed from it those ideas that seemed useful. By borrowing some ideas from Western civilization, the Indians of the 1970's had become different from their predecessors, but they were still unique in many ways.

Borrowing elements from other societies was not something new for most Indian groups. For example, the Navajo people of the Southwest borrowed the idea of farming from Pueblo groups along the Rio Grande in the 1500's. In the 1700's the Navajos borrowed the practice of sheep raising from the Spanish. The Navajos and most of the other Indian groups in the Southwest also borrowed silverwork techniques from the Spanish. Many different Indian groups in the Plains, particularly those in the western Plains, learned from the Spanish how to domesticate horses. This borrowed knowledge ultimately changed the Plains Indians' whole way of life.

In borrowing ideas from American society, Indian groups were careful to select only those ideas that would be beneficial; all others were rejected. *Selective borrowing* produced some interesting results. For instance, some Indian groups incorporated certain Christian symbols into their traditional ceremonies. Similarly, some Indians have begun to use synthetic fabrics and plastics in the manufacture and construction of traditional products.

Television receivers are often present in houses built according to ancient designs.

Selective borrowing has occasionally been crucial to the Indians' survival. One case in point is that of a successful tribally owned factory on one of the Sioux reservations. According to writer Stan Steiner,

> Every Sioux in the factory has his own desk. He comes to work when he wishes. He goes home when he wishes. He will work for twenty-four hours, round the clock, if he wishes; and then he won't work for a week. . . . He is paid at the end of the month for the work he has done, if he has done his work. No one asks him how, or when. He does not have to punch a time clock. There is none. . . . There are no management-labor problems; for management and labor are both the same tribal entity.

Indians are not hard and fast enemies of industry, but many are not willing to assume all of the work habits accepted by most American factory workers. The Sioux realized that informal work procedures were best for them. This decision made their existence more comfortable and secure.

Elements of American government have also been borrowed selectively. Some Indian groups have applied the principles of American politics to tribal problems. For example, local leaders are now frequently elected by group members. But in groups in which clans are important, voting is often conducted on the basis of clan membership, not on the basis of the platforms of the candidates. The voters, thus, are not really electing individuals; they are instead electing kinship groups to various positions. Indians borrowed the principle of electing their leaders, but they have done so without permitting it to disturb the foundations of their societies.

The North American Indians, through group pride, Pan-Indianism, and selective borrowing, entered the 1970's with dignity and strength. They were not, of course, precisely the same kinds of people who had populated America two hundred, or even one hundred years earlier, but the cultural heritage of the past still persisted. These people, as their ancestors had done many years before, had adapted to a new world and a new environment. The environment of the United States was in many respects a severe one. Indians were persecuted unrelentingly by white settlers and their government for two centuries. Yet they managed to endure.

One example of selective borrowing—
a Navajo wagon, pulled by a horse
but mounted on rubber automobile tires.

LASTING CONTRIBUTIONS OF THE INDIANS

Indians have made a significant contribution to the development of American society. Indian customs and practices affected agricultural development, technology, food habits, language, religion, and philosophy. For example, cotton was a crop important to many Indian societies long before the arrival of the Europeans. The corn-belt region of the United States possibly would not exist in its present form if American Indians had not discovered and developed corn as an agricultural crop. Tobacco, potatoes, squash, tomatoes, peanuts, and pumpkins are among the other farm products Indians introduced to European settlers. Indians kept turkeys for food and showed settlers techniques for raising them.

In technology, Indian contributions appear in the manufacture of cloth and pottery and of gold, silver, and copper products. Dams, canals, and other irrigation devices of the Indian groups were copied by white settlers, particularly in the arid Southwest. The canoe, certain kinds of fish traps, and hunting and fishing techniques were also part of the Indians' contribution to "American" technology. The sod hut, the adobe house, and various kinds of timber structures were introduced to white settlers by Indians. Europeans also learned about rubber from the Indians.

The English language now includes hundreds of words derived from Indian sources. Among them are names for foods, such as succotash, squash, hominy, and pecan; names for animals, such as chipmunk, opossum, skunk, moose, raccoon, and woodchuck; and other familiar words, such as hickory, toboggan, mackinaw, and tomahawk. Many names of states, such as Illinois, Massachusetts, Minnesota, Connecticut, Utah, and Delaware are taken from Indian languages. And when names were given to cities and town, ideas frequently came from Indian words. Consider, for example, such names as Chicago, Miami, Tucson, Tacoma, Omaha, Wichita, and Peoria.

Indians also influenced philosophy and thought in the United States. Men such as Ralph Waldo Emerson and Henry David Thoreau were deeply impressed by Indian life. Thoreau, for instance, pointed out that the American people could learn a great deal from the Indians. He observed that the Indian

stands free and unconstrained in Nature, is her inhabitant and not her guest, and wears her easily and gracefully. But the civilized man has the habits of the house. His house is a prison, in which he finds himself oppressed and confined, not sheltered and protected.

Indian thoughts, ideas, and philosophies have been the focus of many studies, especially in recent years. The intent of many of these studies was to encourage people in the United States to re-examine their own ideas.

The influence of the Indians on the actual settlement of America has been significant. Indians provided the European explorers with gifts and information, and they helped the early settlers to survive on the New England coast. Indian trails were used by frontiersmen, and Indians acted as guides and scouts when settlers moved west.

The positive and constructive influence of the Indians on American society undoubtedly will continue and, depending on the attitude of the United States, may increase in the future. By the 1970's there was an indication that relations might well improve. For example, former Secretary of the Interior Stewart Udall, a non-Indian deeply concerned with the problems of land use, wrote that

the conservation movement finds itself turning back to ancient Indian land ideas, to the Indian understanding that we are not outside of nature, but of it. . . . From this wisdom we can learn how to conserve the best parts of our continent. In recent decades we have slowly come back to some of the truths that Indians knew from the beginning: that unborn generations have a claim on land equal to our own; that men need to learn from nature, to keep an ear to the earth, and to replenish their spirits in frequent contacts with animals and wild land. And most important of all, we are recovering a sense of reverence for the land.

Conservationists were among the first Americans who gave serious consideration to the way in which Indians had approached similar problems. They were not by any means alone. Physicians and psychiatrists sensitive to the intricate balance between mental and physical disorders began to investigate the role of medicine men, or shamans, in Indian societies. People concerned with relationships between human values and human behavior began to show a new interest in the religious teachings of different Indian groups. Those concerned with social control and social harmony examined Indian social organizations.

The Indians in North America perhaps have more reason than any other group to regard the United States with distrust, bitterness, and even hatred. Few people in the history of mankind have undergone a longer period of persecution. That they will preserve their cultural identity and self-pride in years to come is hardly questioned. Whether they will do so in an atmosphere of fellowship and good will is the important question.

SUGGESTED FURTHER READING

Deloria, Vine, Jr., *Custer Died for Your Sins.* New York: Macmillan, 1969.

Deloria, Vine, Jr., *We Talk, You Listen.* New York: Macmillan, 1970.

Farb, Peter, *Man's Rise to Civilization.* New York: E. P. Dutton & Co., 1968.

Josephy, Alvin M., Jr., *The Indian Heritage of America.* New York: Alfred A. Knopf, 1968.

Steiner, Stan, *The New Indians.* New York: Harper & Row, Publishers, 1968.

Washburn, Wilcomb E., *Red Man's Land, White Man's Law.* New York: Charles Scribner's Sons, 1971.

BIBLIOGRAPHY

PREHISTORIC INDIANS

Hibben, Frank C., *The Lost Americans,* rev. ed. New York: Thomas Y. Crowell, 1968.
Jennings, Jesse D., *Prehistory of North America.* New York: McGraw-Hill, 1968.
Martin, Paul S., *et al., Indians Before Columbus.* Chicago: University of Chicago Press, 1947.
Wormington, Hannah Marie, *Ancient Man in North America.* Denver: Denver Museum of Natural History, 1957.

AMERICAN INDIAN SOCIETIES

Driver, Harold E., *Indians of North America.* Chicago: University of Chicago Press, 1961.
McNickle, D'Arcy, *The Indian Tribes of the United States.* London and New York: Oxford University Press, 1962.
Wissler, Clark, *Indians of the United States.* New York: Doubleday, 1940.

AMERICAN INDIAN HISTORY

McNickle, D'Arcy, *They Came Here First.* Philadelphia: Lippincott, 1949.
Spicer, Edward H., *A Short History of the Indians of the United States.* New York: Van Nostrand Reinhold, 1969.
Underhill, Ruth M., *Red Man's America.* Chicago: University of Chicago Press, 1953.

CONTEMPORARY AMERICAN INDIANS

Brophy, William A., and Sophie D. Aberle, *The Indian: America's Unfinished Business.* Norman, Oklahoma: University of Oklahoma Press, 1969.
Deloria, Vine, Jr., *Custer Died for Your Sins.* New York: Macmillan, 1969.
Deloria, Vine, Jr., *We Talk, You Listen.* New York: Macmillan, 1970.
Fey, Harold E., and D'Arcy McNickle, *Indians and Other Americans.* New York: Harper & Row, 1959.
Steiner, Stan, *The New Indians.* New York: Harper & Row, 1968.

INDIANS OF THE EASTERN WOODLANDS

Hagan, William T., *The Sac and Fox Indians*. Norman, Oklahoma: University of Oklahoma Press, 1958.

Hickerson, Harold, *The Chippewa and Their Neighbors*. New York: Holt, Rinehart & Winston, 1970.

Hyde, George E., *Indians of the Woodlands from Prehistoric Times to 1725*. Norman, Oklahoma: University of Oklahoma Press, 1969.

Quimby, George I., *Indian Life in the Upper Great Lakes, 11,000 B.C. to A.D. 1800*. Chicago: University of Chicago Press, 1960.

Trelease, Allen W., *Indian Affairs in Colonial New York*. Ithaca, New York: Cornell University Press, 1960.

Wallace, Anthony, F. C., *King of the Delawares: Teedyuscung, 1700–1763*. Philadelphia: University of Pennsylvania Press, 1949.

Wilson, Edmund, *Apologies to the Iroquois*. New York: Farrar, Straus and Giroux, 1960.

INDIANS OF THE SOUTHEAST

Corkran, David H., *The Creek Frontier, 1540–1783*. Norman, Oklahoma: University of Oklahoma Press, 1967.

Cotterill, Robert S., *The Southern Indians: The Story of the Civilized Tribes Before Removal*. Norman, Oklahoma: University of Oklahoma Press, 1954.

Starkey, Marion L., *The Cherokee Nation*. New York: Knopf, 1946.

Swanton, John R., *Early History of the Creek Indians and Their Neighbors*, Bulletin 73. Washington, D.C.: Bureau of American Ethnology, 1922.

Swanton, John R., *The Indians of the Southeastern United States*, Bulletin 137. Washington, D.C.: Bureau of American Ethnology, 1946.

INDIANS OF THE GREAT PLAINS

Berthrong, Donald J., *The Southern Cheyennes*. Norman, Oklahoma: University of Oklahoma Press, 1963.

Denig, Edwin T., and John C. Ewers, eds., *Five Indian Tribes of the Upper Missouri: Sioux, Arickaras, Assiniboines, Crees, Crows*. Norman, Oklahoma: University of Oklahoma Press, 1961.

Ewers, John C., *The Blackfeet: Raiders on the Northwestern Plains*. Norman, Oklahoma: University of Oklahoma Press, 1958.

Hoebel, E. Adamson, *The Cheyennes: Indians of the Great Plains*. New York: Holt, Rinehart & Winston, 1960.

Hyde, George E., *Indians of the High Plains*. Norman, Oklahoma: University of Oklahoma Press, 1959.

Lowie, Robert, *The Crow Indians*. New York: Farrar, Straus and Giroux, 1935.

Mathews, John Joseph, *The Osages: Children of the Middle Waters*. Norman, Oklahoma: University of Oklahoma Press, 1961.

Newcomb, William Wilmon, Jr., *The Indians of Texas from Prehistoric to Modern Times*. Austin, Texas: University of Texas Press, 1961.

Sonnichsen, Charles L., *The Mescalero Apaches*. Norman, Oklahoma: University of Oklahoma Press, 1958.

Wallace, Ernest, and E. Adamson Hoebel, *The Comanches: Lords of the South Plains*. Norman, Oklahoma: University of Oklahoma Press, 1952.

INDIANS OF THE INTERMOUNTAIN REGION

Downs, James Francis, *Two Worlds of the Washo*. New York: Holt, Rinehart & Winston, 1966.

Josephy, Alvin M., Jr., *The Nez Percé Indians and the Opening of the Northwest*. New Haven: Yale University Press, 1965.

Spier, Leslie, *Klamath Ethnography*. Berkeley: University of California Press, 1930.

Stern, Theodore, *The Klamath Tribe: A People and Their Reservation*. Seattle: University of Washington Press, 1965.

Trenholm, Virginia C., and Maurine Carley, *The Shoshonis: Sentinels of the Rockies*. Norman, Oklahoma: University of Oklahoma Press, 1964.

INDIANS OF THE PACIFIC COAST REGION

Barnett, Homer G., *The Coast Salish of British Columbia*. Eugene, Oregon: University of Oregon Press, 1955.

Heizer, Robert F., and M. A. Whipple, eds., *The California Indians: A Sourcebook*. Los Angeles: University of California Press, 1971.

Kroeber, Alfred Louis, *Handbook of the Indians of California*, repr. of earlier edn. Berkeley: California Book Company, 1970.

Ray, Verne F., *Primitive Pragmatists: The Modoc Indians of Northern California*. Seattle: University of Washington Press, 1963.

Rohner, Ronald P., and Evelyn C. Rohner, *The Kwakiutl, Indians of British Columbia*. New York: Holt, Rinehart & Winston, 1970.

INDIANS OF THE SOUTHWEST

Basso, Keith, *The Cibeque Apache*. New York: Holt, Rinehart & Winston, 1970.

Dozier, Edward P., *Hano: A Tewa Indian Community in Arizona*. New York: Holt, Rinehart & Winston, 1966.

Dozier, Edward P., *The Pueblo Indians of North America*. New York: Holt, Rinehart & Winston, 1970.

Forbes, Jack D., *Apache, Navajo, and Spaniard*. Norman, Oklahoma: University of Oklahoma Press, 1965.

Joseph, Alice, *et al.*, *The Desert People: A Study of the Papago Indians.* Chicago: University of Chicago Press, 1949.

Kluckhohn, Clyde, and D. C. Leighton, *The Navajo*, rev. ed. by Lucy H. Wales and Richard Kluckhohn. Garden City, New York: Doubleday, 1962.

Opler, Morris, *Apache Odyssey: A Journey Between Two Worlds.* New York: Holt, Rinehart & Winston, 1969.

Spicer, Edward H., *Cycles of Conquest.* Tucson: University of Arizona Press, 1962.

INDEX

Dakota Indians, 57, 58
Dawes Act, 87
De las Casas, Bartolomé, 32
Delawares, 24, 31, 37, 50, 51, 55
Descent groups, 10–11, 12, 14
De Soto, Hernando, 42

Economic Opportunity Act, 103
Education, 94, 104; agricultural, 54; boarding schools, 82–84, 92, 94; Economic Opportunity Act, 103; government programs, rejection by Indians, 54–56, 78, 79–81; missionaries and church groups, 54–55, 71, 77, 79–80, 82–84; Navajo, contemporary, 111–12; Reorganization Act, 96
Eisenhower, Dwight D., 102
Emerson, Ralph Waldo, 126
Emmons, Glenn, 101
Employment, 99, 104
Encomienda system, 32–33
England: aid to frontier Indians, 51; alliances, 23–24; Cherokees and, 42–47; colonies, 27–31, 36–37, 42; Indian policy, 28–31, 35–38; Spain and, 44; territorial claims, 54; trade, 22, 36, 43–44, 46, 58; War of 1812, 53
Environment, adaptation to, 3–5, 16–17
Explorers, European, 17, 19–22, 58, 61, 126

Farming, 4–5, 9, 14, 31, 40–41, 54, 62, 90, 97, 126
Flatheads, 60, 100
Fort Laramie Treaty, 67
France: alliance, 23; Cherokees and, 42–47; colonies, 27, 28, 42; explorers, 20–21; Indian policy, 33–35; trade, 22–23, 33–35, 43–44, 46, 58; wars, 33–34, 37–38
French and Indian War, 37–38, 46
Frobisher, Martin, 27

Gadsden Purchase, 63
General Allotment Act and policy, 87–89, 90–94
Ghost Dance movement, 91

Gold, 58, 62, 63, 73–74, 81
Grant, Ulysses S., 74, 78
Great Britain, see England
Great Plains, 57–60, 66, 89

Harrison, William Henry, 51, 52
Hudson, Henry, 35
Hunters and gatherers, 3–4, 7, 9, 61, 70
Hurons, 22–24, 33–34, 37, 50

Indian Claims Commission, 100
Indian Departments (Continental Congress), 50
Indian Historian, The, 122
Indian Reorganization Act and policy, 96–99
Indian Rights Association, 92
"Indian territory," 57
Institute for Government Research, 93
Interior Department, 65–67, 100
Intermountain West, 60–61, 67, 80–81, 89; Nez Percé, 70–75
Iroquois, League of the, 23–24, 33–34, 37, 50

Jackson, Andrew, 53, 55, 56, 64–65
Jefferson, Thomas, 55
Joseph, Chief, 75

Kansas Indians, 58
Karlsefni, 20
Kearny, Colonel Stephen, 63
Kickapoos, 51
King George's War, 44

Land: allotment policy, 87–89, 90–94, 96; cessions, 95 (map); claims, U.S., 50, 54; "purchase" by Dutch, 35–36; removal policy and, 55–56, 58, 64–65; reservations, see Reservations; seizure by colonists, 28–31; speculation, colonial, 35, 38; treaties, 50–53, 58, 61–67; use rights, traditional Indian, 8, 30
Laws of Burgos, 32
Lewis and Clark expedition, 58, 60, 71